Mind

An Anthology of Poems
Exploring Mental Health Awareness

Copyright Information

Mind

2020

All rights reserved. © 2020

Cover image copyright belongs to Fndesignart

Copyright for all poems within this book belongs to the authors themselves.

This book has been compiled and edited by Poet Spotlight with permission granted to publish the poems within this anthology.

ISBN - 9798611427354

Cover Image

We would like to thank Fndesignart for donating the amazing artwork for the cover of this book. It perfectly suits the theme of the book. If you would like to see more from this artist please check out @fndesignart on Instagram. You can also contact the artist by the following email address fndesignarts@gmail.com

Mind Anthology

Table of Contents

Introduction..10
Dedication..11
In the Darkness..12
I Promise..13
Let Me Help You Hold On..14
The Colour Within..15
Emerge...16
Little by Little Becomes a Lot..17
Untitled...18
Look Past, No Look Past...19
Yen...20
Make This Your Entrance..21
Untitled...22
Lotuses for Saints..23
You Are Not Alone...24
I Failed...25
Untitled...26
Breathe..28
My Shield and Sword..29
Faith...30
Think..31
Baby Steps..32
Eyes Don't Lie...33
Hope..34
Fragments...35
Can you understand?..36

Not Gone, Just Missing	37
Untitled	38
My Diagnostic and Statistical Manual	39
Psychosis	40
Restore	41
Roses and Tulips	42
Untitled	43
My New Home	44
Untitled	45
Untitled	46
Broughton Dr & Hillsborough St	47
Insomnia	48
Untitled	49
Some Days	50
Stay	58
Weakness	59
Untitled	60
Shine a Light	62
The Abyss	63
A Portion of Purpose	64
Untitled	65
Untitled	67
Anxiety is Building	68
Brightest Star	69
Born in the Land of Earth	70
This is Me	72
Untitled	73
Primal Fear	74
Freedom in Hope's Wings	75

Melancholy Ecstasy	76
Life	77
Untitled	78
Untitled	79
Untitled	80
Never Stop Being You	81
More Than a Bad Day	82
Inner Voice	83
Chasing Tranquillity	87
Untitled	89
Untitled	90
The Last Reminder	91
Stronger	92
Untitled	93
Perspective	94
Criminal Minds	95
Untitled	96
Metamorphosis	97
Untitled	98
Falling Blinds	99
Forgiveness	100
The Guest	101
Thank Your Memories	102
The Language of Silence	103
An Exercise in Being Honest with my Monsters	105
Ombre Stories	106
My Phone Lights up in the Shotgun Seat	107
Off the Ledge	108
Untitled	109

Mushroom Clouding	112
My Way Back Home	114
Untitled	115
Dear You	116
Not for the Naked Eye	117
Rise in the East	118
Real Face	119
Facets of Myself	120
Constant Weather in Changing Seasons	121
Hummingbird	122
Red Hibiscus	123
A Note to Anxiety	124
Depression is Real	125
In The Dark	126
My Truth	127
Collaboration	128
Anatomy of OCD	130
Glass Girl	131
Stolen	132
Morning Comes	133
Stronger	135
Untitled	137
POP	138
Void. Flower	139
Self Appraisal	140
Dear Mind of Mine	141
Untitled	142
Darkness Falls	143
Diamond in the Rough	144

I Remembered	145
Reeling	146
She had a Fault of 3	147
The Light Inside	149
Wonder	150
Making of Me	151
Stalemate	152
Untitled	155
No Such Thing as Crazy	156
A Little Reminder	158
Drowning	159
Prism of Hope	160
The Hottest Day	161
A Poem on Mental Health	162
Who I Am	163
Trauma is my Muse	164
Untitled	166
Change the Game	167
An Invitation	169
Simplicity, oddly enough	170
Stop/Start	171
It's All in my Head	172
Grave-ful	173
I Want	174
Smile Once More	175
The World Needs Your Precious Petals	176
Untitled	177
Bitter Words	178
Hearth of Hope	179

Freedom..180
Biographies..181

Introduction

Mental Illness affects so many of us, and many of us have suffered in silence for too long.
It is time to open up and start talking about our suffering, so we may seek help.
Poetry has long been a way of giving life to our emotions and opening up about our pain.
This book brings poetry and mental health awareness together, in a way that is relatable, but also hopeful and insightful.
We hope you, dear reader find some comfort in these words when the darkness is all consuming we hope this may give a little light to help you find your way.
This poetry anthology is a collection of poems by over 100 poets from the Instagram community.
I would like to thank each and every one of the amazing poets in this book for making this project a reality.
100% of the profits from this book will be going to Mind Charity.

Dedication

This book is dedicated to all of those
who suffer with mental illness,
you are not alone
and never will be.

In the Darkness

Sometimes it's necessary to hide in the darkness in order to heal your wounds;

a secluded place to comfort your soul while you learn to accept your reality.

Lay in the shallows my darling,
but don't swim too deep.
The bottom of the abyss is where there lies no return to tomorrow.
Sooner or later you must face the light.
Come to the surface.
You can't expect to drown in the darkness forever, if you want to see the sunrise.
Lick the wounds of your tender soul.
Take your time to recover.
I want you to know there's always room for your return.
Faces get lonely without a smile
and the sun longs to shine for you.

~S.R.Chappell
@inkedheartpoetry

I Promise

Your eyes painted with sadness
I stare into their profound emptiness
A complete void of lawlessness
Tangled up, the asphyxiation within
feels like travelling in the vacuum of space
Alone amidst flickering lights, happily dancing
How are they winning?
We're all struggling
But how come they are winning?
Your demons slowly put out your burning desire
Break down your walls leaving you vulnerable
But you know...
We're not going anywhere
You'll rise again
You'll fly again
Our light will shine in the darkened canvas of the sky
Forming a constellation of hope for everyone else
I promise
I won't give up
So don't listen to the melodies of misery
Hell does exist - it's the chaos in our own head
Heaven exists too - it's the soothing acceptance of oneself
Striving to be, and simply
Breathing...
Heaven exists within our soul and we'll find it together
So don't abandon yourself
I promise
We'll make it
I promise.
@archmage_poetry - Vorg

Let Me Help You Hold On

I see you at the end of your rope
I feel that you are giving up hope
I hear your cries of despair
I want you to know that I care
I need you to pick up the phone
To tell you that you are not alone
I would drive miles to be at your door
To hold you until you feel pain no more
Please let some light in
Don't let the darkness win
You have more life left to live
There is nothing that I wouldn't give
To have you here for another day
I can't promise that it will all be okay
But I can promise to help you through
Whatever it is, I am here for you
Reach out. Hold on. Don't give up.

Katherine Elizabeth

@katerinapoetry

The Colour Within

I hope you find the colour
In every black and white day
That beams of light shine right through
Whenever it is dark or grey

I have faith that this will happen
Because of one certainty that is true
You have your very own sunshine
There inside of you

All you need to do is to reveal
The wonder that is you
And all the light and color
Will come flooding back to you

@mynamemeans_perseverance

Emerge

When I sense the surge
the rush of the gush
and I fear that it may drown me
I breathe and I pause
to let my mind see
I can swim and bide
to glide and ride
this scourge of a wave
that used to enslave
and cause anguish
till I grew enough brave
to crush, to slay, and to vanquish

@swellversed

Little by Little Becomes a Lot

Let me sink in the depths of despair
Even to wish I could disappear
Not leaving a single trace of me
Blank pages, missing my history
I'm sinking deeper and cannot swim
Into my lungs water rushes in
No matter the fathoms that I go
I still believe in my tomorrow
I try to be patient with myself
Still always my choice and no one else
Only please stay close, throw me a line
Remind me that life changes take time
Believe in me and hear what I say
Forgive me if I cause pain some days
They say life's not measured by breaths
I'm learning it is all a process
The wrenching lows and exciting highs
Will one day make sense of all the whys
Life is a collective adventure
Moments that take my breath I'll treasure
I'll hold on tight and never let go
I am stronger than I even know
A passioned heart, I feel things deeply
Roar loud life's not meant to be easy
Keep my mind strong in those crazy times
When I feel low and my mind's offline
I'll read a book, try to help someone
Little by little my fights being won

@nobullheart

Untitled

My heart is heavy
Stumbling to make light
Of this load I carry
Try as I might, I've lost sight
Of everything good and bad
All I bone crushingly feel
Is overwhelmingly sad
Soul laid brutally bare
I'm spluttering on stagnant air
Hankering to pack up
Monotony of trouble and strife
Bid a final farewell to
this shell of a life
I pull myself back
From this one track
Way of thinking
Lord God help me
How can I continue
Avoiding Satan winking

@maiamusings

Look Past, No Look Past

You, my love hold no past,
And you, my love tolerate us all;
Tell me what happened in your past life?
Do you remember and is it
Your call to fame,
With a memory vivid in the
Depths of it all.
Rain came in the window
Of the tram,
I believe it was forty-five drops
I felt.
All along, with on and on,
And on, and on.
You didn't say your part
Contribute to art,
The façade was almost hidden
By the trees.
The silence was golden,
It was enjoyed by everyone.
Even the voices
Inside the head of me.

@thepoetshove

Yen

And he asked me,
"Don't you sulk?
And I said,
"I want to!"
"What stops you then?"
Probed he.
"A mollifier!" Muttered I.
"A mollifier?"
He seemed perplexed!
"A lack of one!" I cried.
He looked at me so baffled
A quizzical look he gave
I wondered if he'd descended
My spirit, My soul to save!
I felt at home and poured
Pent up feelings within
And told him how I craved
To brood, to pout, to pine!
I desiderated someone -
To come and hold my hand
Cajole me into smiling with love's magic wand.
Of words and gestures loving
Just the way I do
I long to hear the same
To rid me of the blue!
But what is fate's design?
None can fathom or gauge,
Laughter and love fill many lives
Yet others- a mere blank page.

Latika Ojha. @penned_passion

Make This Your Entrance

It's happening again
For the third time.
I have tried so many times
To die
But it promises this will be
The final attempt.
This will be the end.
It plans it in my mind
Elaborately,
Telling me it will be
Mid-dream, mid-fantasy.
The exit sign shines
And I can see a bed of tulips behind it.
The bus finally arrives
And this will be the last time.
The transformation will be
Into one of a butterfly.
It whispers,
'Your wings for once
Will not be broken.'
It's happening again
For the third time.
I have tried so many times
To die
And now I scream in its face.
I tear up its plans,
I lock them in a case.
I tell it my life
Can be a dream, a fantasy.
The entrance sign shines
And I can see a bed of tulips behind it.
The bus finally arrives
And this will happen
Many more times.
The transformation will be
Into one of a butterfly.
I scream,
'Death will not give me wings,
I can fly in this life.

@liv3thr0ughthispoetry

Untitled

I understand now.
Walking, eating salad cannot make it better.
Stopping feeling, won't change me. It's in the grey matter.
Always circling, deeply critical. I'm in my skull now.
Non neurotypical. Locked up, tied down.
Ever outside, burning words try to make deals.
But it's late, I'm stranded on the ferris wheel.
Thinking click like gangster, tongue sword like medical.
Exact tax fanatical, pieces just gone.
I hate who I have become.
I don't see me in the mirror.
I cramp in my hand, jaw locking, I stop talking.
I am now the burden, traffic you might need to detour.
I need to save you the trouble. Let you be you and not call.
This sickness parietal. I am unsure now. I am dull.
Wounded, bent and stunted. I have no capacity. I play dead.
Fresh air is nothing, has no effect.
I feel the eyes coming back, my insight spurt, rapid attack.
I can't open doors more than a crack. Subtle aura instant.
I fade, I don't come back.
I am scared of my face. Horrified by my body.
Mind just elevates. Blind hatred for me.
I need you to go. So I can become the arrow.
To fly true, the pact made in December.
It just seems so real, like I'm not a heart you can heal.
I cannot force field or up shield. There is too much now.
I just don't remember. And every moment that's passing me.
Glares icy. The final question repeats.
Why now? Why are you still here?

@wordsthatburnedpoetry

Lotuses for Saints

To covet the Kardashians with pay-offs in a modern brand,
Curmudgeons with carnelians and chaos for the common man,
Dare to wish a winter died with its life first remembered,
Where we fish the rivers dry as the skies burn in embers,
Stare permissions in the eye as the lights turn to cinders,
Share a kiss with pictures pried from the white kernels rendered,
Sold a smile like a lamp with the rocks white and pictures red,
Hold the child by the hand as you walk by the riverbed,
Bring the coatless to the heat in the peace of the view there,
Leave a lotus on a leaf like a liege at the Louvre,
Summon thousands on a beach they emerge and arrive,
From the mountains to the reefs with the birds where they fly!

@bigsalpoetry

You Are Not Alone

Your pains are not your own
Don't hide in memories repress
Share them, you are not alone
Sorrow, don't cage to suppress

Into corner deep don't store to keep
Thoughts that ache and agony give
Pen them down or to someone speak
Help soul to heal the grieve

When sadness crumples you
And darkness speaks with you
Don't let this give you the blue
Just remember family loves you

When illness does give sorrow
And you feel the world end
With no happiness in tomorrow
Just remember to call a friend

Don't give home to sadness
Don't make it so dear
Search for the little happiness
Make strength to live and kill fear

@wordsadrifting

I Failed

Yes, I failed
In learning,
In understanding,
In performing;
Yes, I failed
In something an ordinary
person
Never fails;
Yes, I failed
In being part of
a their population,
'A Normal one';
Where everyone is
somewhat caught up in
their own
Feelings, emotions,
Expectations, and other
self motives,
Where they understand
but don't comprehend,
Where they operate
but don't co-operate,
Where they speak
but don't talk,
And still they think
they are normal;
But I say
Yes, I am not normal
No one is.

Akshita Agrawal

@wordsdepth

Untitled

Stuck in my throat
Choking, gagging
On my own voice
Invisible hands
Of my own making
Brain cried, tried
No relief
White pill
No thrill
Just chill
But still
Shhhhh
Gone are days
Of
Getting gone
Going long
Natural fun
Freedooooom
Now chained
Restrained
Bound & tied
Christian Gray says this is fun?
Guess I'm not that type of girl.
Can't breathe
Release me
Please
Light fading
Legs wading
Through water
To my waist
Now shoulders
Floating
Sounds muffled
Eyes flutter
The dark
But not
Because
Buzzing thoughts
Blaring voices
Start again
Yet I'm still
Captive
To
My
Anxiety

My brains
Self imposed
Straight jacket
I don't get to pick the color
It just comes in
Oh fuck here we go again
And I'm trying to hold back tears
Because don't ugly cry in public
Find an exit
Deer in headlights
The initial drop
I can hear the train
See the light
This is the game
Can I move in time
Or
Do I collapse
On the floor
I see it in my head
Spotlight on my heap
People walk around
Here is my melancholy solo
Mere seconds have passed
Yet my panic
Full blown
Full grown
Full Godzilla
Screaming, shaking Tokyo size
In seconds
This is my panic
This is my anxiety
This is what I will beat
But for now I'm a little
Dramatic

@kayt_of_wands

Kayt Rozdzek

Breathe

In the broken moments
The moments when you feel you will never heal

The moments when you are burning with emotion and the gold won't set in your cracks
The moments when a butterfly's colours don't bring joy, but envy because they taste a freedom you will never get
The moments when your flame dips and shakes fighting against the hurricane of your shadows
The moments when you are afraid to breathe, because anyone deserves that air more than you
The moments when the sheets become your world because anything outside of your bed is too much
The moments when you catch your reality in between your chewed and broken fingernails and don't recognise it
The moments when you are sharp, where you should be soft and you try to file down your edges with lacerated thoughts
The moments when signs and life are hazy in the mists of mistrust
The moments when you piece together the shards of broken memories, wondering what is happening to you
The moments you cry until your chest heaves with exhaustion and your ribs ache from protecting your heart
Those broken moments
And so many more
Are real
Are valid
Those moments bring us to our knees
In those broken moments
Please
Breathe

By Sky Rose Heywood @skyroseheywood

My Shield and Sword

With this shield and sword.
I vow to do my
best.

To help make this
a better world
and clean up
a part of this
mess

My paper and my pen, on these
I can depend

To write the
wrongs in some peoples
eyes

Even if it brings
out a few
cries

The shield and sword are
powerful in the moment, not sure
for how much
time

But my pen and paper give
me the power
to make
rhyme

For in this
digital world
these words
may reach
another

And he may
become my
brother

@jessmischke

Faith

A rare moment of clarity,
A chance for me,
A future to see,
In my pursuit to find a happy me.
Amongst the days that hold me back,
Behind the storms that paint me black,
There shines a light so very bright,
That illuminates my entire sight.
This is why I will not fade,
This light's the reason that I've stayed,
I know it's not always easy to see,
But I know in my heart that it shines for me.
It's shines of hope and a chance of peace,
It shines of a future where my worries cease,
It shines to show me what can come true,
And if you care to look,
It will shine for you.

@gift_of_poetry

Think

I think I'm starting to believe/ I should stop to believe my thoughts / and start to think how to retrieve / my starts when I stop at a loss

@niels_shoenmaker

Baby Steps

You tell me you are broken
You tell me you need help
Desperate words are spoken
A torrent of self doubt

I answer you are young
With many years to learn
Countless songs unsung
Bridges yet to burn

You tell me you feel restless
Unsure which path to follow
You are feeling lost and clueless
Emptied out and hollow

I remind you that you're a student
And life is still your classroom
It takes time to be life fluent
To create your personal theme tune

You are poetry in motion
A masterpiece in progress
In line for the next promotion
Baby steps to awesomeness

@shandrewspoetry

Eyes Don't Lie

Your eyes tell a story
They cannot lie
Your upbeat facade
Cannot hide, you
Are wounded, hurting
Scars they ache
Beneath your duvet with
Darkness in your wake
A geyser of red
Gushes within me
As my heart implodes
At your plight
I feel your torment, your every sigh
It makes me want to curl up and die
I can't bear to see the deep dejection
Seeping through those windows blue
Reach out and comfort you
Is all that I want to do..
Bring a smile to your face
However fleeting and in my embrace
Chase the shadows far away
Hold you near
Whisper softly in your ear...
A lullaby, a simple tune
To exorcise the demons in the room
Lift the cloud, watch it fade
Never to return another day.

J.E. @julesielle

Hope

Never leave me
The thought of better days
Giving me strength always
Lifting dark clouds away

You are always with me
Telling me things are okay
Reassuring my heart and head
I know you are here to stay

Sometimes I can't see you
But still I know you're there
When my heart is tired and weary
And I feel I just don't care

As surely as the sun appears
From a dark and cloudy sky
My spirit starts to rise again
And you help me to get by

No one can take you from me
For we will never part
I just can't live without you
You live inside my heart

@carol_longfellow

Fragments

She felt like doing nothing yesterday
She felt like doing everything today
Love her on both days

@livvywritespoetry

Can you understand?

I am over it...
I have been there, done that..
That's what says my stats
This anxiety, this panic attack
PPD is getting hard to crack

Those looks make me confused
I cannot learn to refuse
I need something to diffuse
I wanna go so badly, Can you excuse?

Growing pressure of rejection
Screw this dejection
Catalysts to my addiction
And in addition,

Pinching myself, clenching my teeth
Is this the proper way to treat?
Please you all, Let me breathe,
I wanna scream and go out in the street

You said, I was not being social
You said, I am getting so emotional
You said, I am too vocal
You said, don't be so sentimental
My story is not sensational

Don't you know, what's going on in me!
Oh lord! can you ever set me free?
Tired of making everybody "Happy"
Tired of being "Miss Yes"
Can't you see?

Head spinning, body aching
Trembling and shaking
Its just too much to take in
Now my mind starts interrogating

I feel that you are not here
I feel that you are not fair
Delusional mind, but who cares.
Relations on the edge of break up and tear
@confessions_of_sophia

Not Gone, Just Missing

Where the frost lays upon the ground
And icicles hang all around
Where you know the sun won't shine,
And life won't grow through earth or vine,
Where breath is foggy and the view is frozen,
You search for warmth in each emotion,
Where the birds have flown and cocoons save life,
And fortune hangs like a thread on a knife,
Where the fire won't take and you ache for the flame,
Death won't come for you nor life just the same,
The in-between isolation of a turning circle,
Blood so stagnant it becomes curdled,
Through that darkness, that frozen air,
A light still shining an endless flare,
I'm reaching toward it, but the distance seems a lifetime away,
Hope still flickers as I try to find a way,
I pray to the cosmos and any god, any one that will listen,
They don't give up, I'm not gone, just missing.

@crumpledheart2019

Untitled

I'm sitting across from the person hiding inside me
My depression
It's telling me to give up
Telling me to end it now.
But I'm stronger than that.
I don't listen to them.
Because without them.
I'm just me.
A happy version of myself
But my depression stands up
And starts to throw punches
It's starting to make me weak.
It's knows what it's doing
It knows that there is a point where I will give in
A point where no matter how hard I fight them
They will always win.
And right now that's where I am
I'm weak.
It takes all my strength to get out of bed
And to go to school
And to put on a smiling face
To pretend it's all okay
But that's my version of fighting back.
No matter how hard my depression tries
Tries to take me down
I always get back up
My depression will never get the best of me.
Not this time

@l_ove_letters

My Diagnostic and Statistical Manual

Feeling trapped within a seam
Thoughts and words from a distant dream
The salient aspects of the day
Suddenly have faded to gray
Intangibly or just beyond the clear
To hope, I can no longer adhere
For the circuit board of my mind
Has been caught up in a fuzzy bind
This cannot be happening to me
Bleakness blankets, all I see
I am lost and need to be found
Within a sad story is where I'm bound
Remove the dust cover and peek inside
Alas, a gleam of light for depression's lonesome bride

@stacy_coventry_is_here

Psychosis

PSYCHOSIS
Is when
Your mind plays
Sick games and your
MADDENING
Thoughts think
They are real
Sinking you into a
HOLE
Of desperation
You become
Depressed from not
Wanting to live any
MORE.

@mariawyn316

Restore

As we live, we fill ourselves with the iniquities,
whether we may have done it,
Knowingly or unintentionally.
Yet, we have scratched our soul with them.
We have partaken into the misery
where we would just sit and mourn
for what we had done, or
what we could have.
But then, to restore,
isn't in our hands.
We, only can let God and time,
to restore us back to,
as we had wished to be.
Though, we rightly know,
What's gone, can't be amended.
But, at least we can be normal.
We can never get away from the iniquities,
But, at least we can try to reduce them.
While asking the almighty to,
help us to achieve them.

@flexonpaulpoetry

Roses and Tulips

Roses and Tulips started to bloom,
blooming within silent tombs
flowers and their lovely fumes,
hiding beneath their smiling masks and costumes

Rebuilding the society,
with the purpose of regaining equality,
amplified voices of every soul in this land, flowing like electricity,
echoing within every race and nationality

Plucking the petals, tainted with layers of oppression
Grit can be seen on their facial expressions
Society's inequality and suppression,
filled men and women with transgression

Silvery dews dripping from their fingertips,
"Plink! Plink! Plink!" as it drips,
Love written on their scarlet lips,
flowers trapped in a society with venomous grips

Individuality and diversity tattooed on their sleeves,
Their voices scattered among fallen leaves,
Embracing and capturing the light like daring thieves,
Standing strong, breaking stereotypes even if nobody believes

We are Jewels covered with sunflower petals and succulent leaves

@blcklns_aj18

Untitled

Depression...
A word said by millions
Millions not saying a word

@wordsfrom1985

My New Home

If you ever wanna go to Hell, just let me know. You can stay in my room. It's on the right to the left of the sign-in table, down below, underneath the stairwell. Just look for the sign that I hung up above with a hangman's noose, with 'My Beautiful,' loosely written across the top. In fact, I just got back. The good news is, there's no mess to clean up this time, no blood left behind, no more scars on my arms that I need to hide. I already fucked myself up enough in this current life of mine, but that's not the reason why I went back inside.

I needed to look around. I needed to find what was wrong. I needed to know what it was that's been pulling me down. What's been causing this aggression, this depression, this overwhelming passion for self-destruction! I needed to ask my internal assassin who's always been faithful, riding shotgun every time I would run, telling no-one that I wanted to be done with all of this shit, so you won't miss me just in case I didn't come back. Like I said, in fact, I just did! I'm right here! Me and my backpack of self-inflicting paradigms fully intact with salvation in my eyes.

I'm sure there's a few if not more than many, who will be disappointed to learn of my re-entry. That's okay. I'm used to that. I'm just an asshole in a paper hat. But when I went into visit my old friend, Depression said that it wasn't him I was looking for. That Sadness had returned stronger than before. Now that I know, now that I'm back, now that I can get my life back on track. There's something you should know that I'm finally ready to say, there's something I did before I went away, before I left, I tied that hangman's noose around my waist instead of my neck. I did it so if I was gone too long, that you'll be able to find me! Why? Because I finally have a family I want to come home to. Who you say? All of you....

@bryan.edwards.live

Untitled

There is always a time to make things right, and a time when things do fall into place. You think, you overthink but thinking does not lead you anywhere. Your actions do. And now, you're moving in the right direction. The best part is you're fully aware of the circumstances you find yourself in and you are now, slowly and steadily taking steps to improve your situation. Rather if I may say – you're moving away from the problems and you're moving inwards, towards your true self; your solution is right inside you. You explore and search outside for what can fix you, your fears, your anxieties, issues which you face with yourself - but that fix is inside you. It is only a matter of time, that you realize that one human being cannot be a problem - he/she can only be a solution. Hence, so are you. Your weaknesses are your strengths and all you need to do is channelize (what you think is) your problem into a solution. Our weaknesses should never be a hindrance to a life we deserve - we often do not realise that. And most of the time, when it's too late. Realising what one has hidden inside is the true purpose of every human being. It is a waste of life if one does not realise one's worth. Even if a lot of people throw stones at you on the way up - it does not mean you deserve them. The stones in your path and the slaps on your face should remind you what you're capable of. Those test your resilience and patience - they will always bring you out stronger. One should always remember - the failures, the hardships are proof that you're moving, that you're alive and you have place reserved only for you - empty and waiting. It is only your right to that reservation - and only you will fill it.

@so.i.ar

Untitled

I don't know how many times I have almost given up,
Hit rock bottom and told myself. "I am done"
Every time I have done that, something within has always pulled me back,
Back to shape like a drawn rubber band, taut one second, free the next...

I have given up so many times, that I have lost count.
Overwhelmed with guilt, shame and helplessness,
A train of thoughts of nothing and everything at the same time.

Its gotten too tiring, sapping every ounce of my energy to even breathe,
I have chugged along like old age, just about rolling over each day,
Ticking them off the calendar and sulking even more.

Shrugged shoulders, droopy eyes, dejected faces,
Buckled ankles, wobbly knees have come many times,
But a mad voice and spirit has come even more.
"Go on for one more day, one more hour, one more second"

I've let go of toxic ideas, toxic people and dangerous thoughts,
I have learnt to laugh, to endure rough patches,
I have learnt to love myself more.
I have learnt to trust life and stay alive.

I have given up on paths, people, relationships and what not.
Hit the abyss like a brick train.
I have survived nightmares, panic attacks and loneliness.
I have not given up on fighting when it has been so easy to accept the easy way out.

I am proud of my struggles,
I am proud of my failures.
They have been quite a rich concoction of disasters.
It has made me who I am.
The man who fights for what he believes in.
I believe in myself.

@sunilsathyendra

Broughton Dr & Hillsborough St

When I am hungry or sleepy,
I sit high in a building that towers
above a bustling, blinding street.

I watch other human beings walk
in and out of restaurants with locked arms. They have
plastic bags full of steamy take-out ripping onto the streets.

The rising steam is pregnant with egg roll, and vegetable taunts me
through thick glass. My stomach is more clamorous than
commute and chatter and it cries silently. I won't listen anyway.

Neon vibes flashing red, yellow, and green float below me,
reminding me that I won't be the only one who's awake the
rest of the night.

I try to distract myself by counting the number of
cracks on each block of sidewalk, or I
pick at the smudges on my window.

I trace my finger over the bags of my throbbing eyes.
At least they are smiling.
My friends each have warm, stitched comforters to hug them tonight.

I must be either powerful enough or delusional enough to
see an ant stumble over fresh french fries on worn asphalt,
as if the ant had its own mountains to climb too.

Published with A Gathering of the Tribes Magazine 2019

@poetic.patricia

Insomnia

I sat in the dark
Listening to sounds
Whispering noises;
On the ceiling
While the shadows
Bounding and leaping;
Mid air
throwing my blanket
on and off
Waving out the window to
The inconsiderate stars, they know me
They are awake with me, yet they are content;
Not me
tiring my eyes in hopes of sleep
as thoughts lovingly
Choke my mind
@momina_writes_

Untitled

My family complains of me being too quite, QUIET?
Too soft in my tone, contrary to my genes.
They want me to be them.
Do they ever feel like I should be me?
Soft to my inner core,
my tongue harsh only against their bullying.

I often sit and stare blank in space,
without any care of where I am or
with whom I am.
Am I the only one who feels like
I'm always more lost than I ever am found?
Am I the only one who believes 'house' is not
always 'home'?

@poetry_in_paris

Some Days

(A 13 poet collaboration)

Some days I struggle to breathe
Some days the darkness hooks it's anchor
In my sore from crying throat
Some days the anchor slips and I can breathe
Some days the anchor pulls me down and lays on top of me

Some days the light is a pin prick
Not a twinkling star, but a too far away bulb
Some days it's barely recognizable
The darkness, it extinguishes me
Some days the escape isn't felt with any of my five senses

Some days I feel this is where I will stay
Locked in this vessel that can't hold my pain
Some days I dangle across the veil of sanity
Peeking to see if there is a way out on that side

But some days
Some days the light expands
Some days the breathing is easy
Some days I see a reason to continue
Some days I see beauty
@skyrosepoetess

When the light of new day peeks up and winks
I lie still, ignoring blue ascension over dark pinks
My bed is my boat and I'm cast off alone
separate from everyone I've ever known

Floating encased in sheets entangled
from disturbed midnight dreams wrangled
Tossing and turning, troubles invading
A silent war which open mind is evading

A sadness clear - so crisp, so tangible
Emotions roll up, then down unmanageable
And still, the sun continues to rise
yellows, oranges sneak into bedroom and eyes

I'm forced to wake, to face the day
to tackle my demons an alternate way
Hush! Hush! Push them down and smile
For the world expects sunshine's masked guile

But little by little as I breathe in the beauty
of a new day, I feel the duty
To live this life, to go on and heal
my one life, this precious vitality that's real

@lindalokheeauthor

Today...
Should be, by all appearances, a good day.
I wrote in my online gratitude journal...
Today.
I performed three guided YouTube meditations,
Repeated one hundred-and-seven positive affirmations
Took selfies while forcing down two kale smoothies,
And group photos, performing hot yoga duties...
Today.
That's proof I experienced joyous ecstasy...
Today.
At least that's what all the
Glowing, skinny Instagram girls,
Enlightened in shining
Patent leather Chanel and Louis Vuitton armor say.
Openly liking memes of self-betterment,
Scrolling the social gorilla glass gaol,
Seething suppressed and secret contempt,
Should I feel content on the inside,
Being dis-connected by cell phone, right alongside
Millennial's, each so unique and unlike me
In the age where we collectively, behind screens, safely rise,
Offended by how we were all traumatized,
And take pride in self-growth-related competition,
Chatting for hours, sitting alone,
Thumbs doing the talking
On voice-activated smartphones,
Throat chakras constrained
In this Ethernet realm where overwhelmingly popular
Opinions on spiritual realization rain abundance?
But I know I have choices, and some days I take a chance,
Switch off, and create, on my own, days that liberate. I dance
Secretly, publicly outdoors in the rain, smiling and singing,
Not captured on camera posing like that and pouting like this.
Instead of swallowing prescribed, virtual spiritual bliss
That feels like swimming in a sea of dead fish and winning,
I choose freedom from healing that chokes and joy that restrains...
Some days.
@eastwest_nomad

Some days I wonder if I'm ever gonna feel
Better like I remember those days the sun fell
Down upon my forehead as I danced and sang
Lofty tunes on top of trees I'd climbed
High on branches standing strong and taller
Than I actually was in my happy childhood
That suppressed so much pain and despair
Sliding through the open door in my adulthood
To unleash its fears and daily scope
Of wishful, maybes, what-ifs somedays.
@reenadossauthor

Sometimes hate is the easiest way out of pain
As red dim bulbs compared to the total darkness,
And I wonder if lightening brightly last torch of hope
Can also be a heartless action.

Sometimes crushing onto a rocky bottom
Breaking lustful thighs and caring hands, and eyes
That once watched with love into another eyes -
Ping-pong balls alike jump out of fragile flesh, now rotten;
Can also be the mercy for the hopeless.

Sometimes good and evil intertwined
Choke me together by the choices I can't make.
Tsunami of past promises I kept and didn't keep -
Too much to comprehend.

Sometimes I am dead inside.
Sometimes I feel alive.
And always I am me with no excuses.
@_geothepoet_

I see the beauty through tearful eyes
And let my heart skip a beat, on hope
Like a Kaleidoscope
Colors spreads and tell lies

Stars are shining little brighter tonight
Flowing with symphonic breeze,
My body finds its own pace,
No dragging it through this time
Cause my chest is confidently tight
All of it is a home of mine

summertime sadness replace Counting stars
Passionate poems and musics scars

Feels like this smile would last
A little longer
Oh please god! Let it stay,
just a little longer

A gush of cold wind
Remind,
All the buried memories inside
@whispersofbrokenheart

The days the fog is out
Some days it's hard to see
Some days, fills me with doubt
And days it's tough to be

Some days the waves, they crash
My boat of hope, ashore
Some days it yells and fights
Making the sounds of war

But some days they are green
And smell of petrichor
Daisies and mountain peaks
Give me strength, they implore

To get up, rise and shine
It's my time. Happy day
Fighting shadows too long
Carefree, it's time to play

That's why, don't fight my dark
With stream we need to flow
I know and trust my Lord
His righteous light will glow...
@rumillenialpoetry

Sometimes I dread
What lays beyond my bed
And the fears take over me

Sometimes I feel
That this life is unreal
I want to set my demons free

Sometimes I wonder
If I hide from the thunder
Caused by the battles in my head

Would I rest in peace
Would the nightmare cease
Would my legs turn back from lead

I'll never know
Unless I go
And put my feet down on the floor

Raise my head up high
Knowing that I tried
Find the courage to go on once more.
@knackeredmummy

As I look back,
it pains me to see myself shrunk,
barely functioning in my full capacity.

This invisible black hole draining my energy,
reducing dragons to touch me not.
Sapping my desires and dulling my zest for life.
I have lost the deal.

Its still a wonder,
that I am even surviving this mind onslaught.
Wave after wave hits me, sadness, happiness
and every other emotion has eroded.
Now it's nothing but emptiness that is left.
An empire of pure and absolute nothingness
that beats even Alexander's prowess.

But there is a tree that grows in all this deserted land.
One last breath of air that still beats for ethics,
that still roars like African lions,
that thrives like active volcanoes.
There is hope.

A hope that another dawn shall bring me back home,
maybe there is a Hansel and Gretel story here somewhere.
Getting me back home in major reset.

Back in time or forwarded to the future
@sunilsathyendra

It's hard to imagine
A place with no light
In darkness so deep
You give up the fight

Just when you think
You can't get any lower
The feeling sinks deeper
And time starts to move slower

That's when you feel it
A tingle in your soul
The fire is burning
To make you feel whole

Never give up
Never lose hope
If you reach out your hand
You can always find a rope.
@roses.are.rob

When the hallucinations meet the realities at the cusp of life,
on the shore of illusion
walkways are soft
on the days I'm awake,
the pathways are sharp.
Sometimes are dark
sometimes life is a fun park.
Sometimes playing harp seems dutiful
But on some days humming freely feels beautiful.
Life is situational
with reel and real tangs
at times it's bangs back
other times it's bountiful pack.
@poetess_sampada

Thriller! Thriller!, chased by an angry gorilla
negativity like a gang of guerillas
invading my mind, turning me into a chinchilla
A prisoner in my own villas

Some days am slipping and stalling
Some days am leaping but falling
Some days am ranting and panting
Some days am wanting but stunting

Screamer! Screamer!, they tell me to be quiet

Imposing on my mind a poisonous diet
Telling me I am immature, not there yet
the monsters on the outside turn me into a pet

Some days I wish someone would just listen
Some days it's only a form of mind frisson
Some days I wish my heart would glisten
Some days it's only a form of mind ricin

Dreamer! Dreamer!, you can not back down now
Swimmer! Swimmer!, you can not drown now
Most days, I will stand tall and fight hard
Most days, I will play ball and rule the yard

'Cos when you get pushed down,
you gotta get up, get up
'Cos when you get crushed now,
you gotta heal up, heal up

'Cos you are a warrior
Can't let nothing worry you
It's okay to cry at the corridor
Don't let the tears bury you
@creozoe_ink

Oh these days that come and go
like ocean waters
with ebbs and flows
that drown out and silence
the screeching echoes

The voices that scream
you're never enough
you'll always be less than
and never add up

The battle consumes
my mind almost daily
dominates my behaviour
and makes my hands shaky

Then that still small voice
within the crashing waves
regards me as a warrior
that I'm mighty to save

So I lift my head

stretch my hands to the sky
slowly go under
a new creation, I arise.
@abbeyforrestauthor

Stay

Someone's world became a better place
because of you.
Someone's life changed for good
because of you.
Strangers, most of them may have been
but no single life is disconnected from another
even when we feel most alone.
Stay
and let the world experience
how much good there still is
that comes from you.

@september.stardust

Weakness

Is it a weakness-
to admit you are the mess-
isn't it easier to then understand
why I recoil at your hand?

Is it a weakness-
to accept the hand of others
and become difficult lovers?
yes- I'll start thinking less.

Is it a weakness-
to admit you are worthless
to assume the world knows this
and who will miss those amiss?

Is it a weakness-
to accept who will be missed?
because it is you my dear
the one who used to live without fear.

Is it a weakness-
to admit you are the mess
or is it just another excuse
for these feelings you refuse?

Maybe because I fear looking into their eyes,
and finding a side I recognize.

@musesofapoet

Untitled

Picking this scab
The instant sting
It seems that pain
Makes my soul sing

Now as this blade
Slices a fresh wound
The symphony in my soul
Has been tuned

The claret river
Flows down my arm
My soul is dancing
To the devil's charm

It seems this time
He has finally won
After this final slice
My after life has begun

My world goes dark
I begin to cower
Standing before me
Three figures of incredible power

One dressed in devilish red
One dressed in silky white
One dressed in pure black
Each make an invite

The devil makes a pitch
Telling me my soul is tainted
I've been tormented for long
And his calling card has been painted

God's pitch is divine and pure
He speaks of salvation
An afterlife of service and atonement
For a reincarnation

Death makes the final plea
He says how he can train me
He'll mould me into death itself
A successor is who I'm meant to be

I take a second to decide
Churning over the bargains
I open my mouth to speak
"I choose" I begin...

@poetdobby

Shine a Light

Here's the thing about silence,
the kind that screams to be known,
longing for a sense of security,
that makes you feel all alone.
The pain washes over you solely,
drenching you until you're numb,
you fight to feel almost anything,
until you become undone.
Depression looms in a nightmare,
it buries right into the core,
scars, tears and heartbreak emerge,
until you can't get up off the floor.
Anxiety crawls on your skin,
an itch that won't go away,
a thing that we call mental health,
is a price you have to pay.
When dark thoughts enter your mind,
shine a light for others this way,
offer out a hand or hug;
and tell them it will be OK
You see love can be found inside,
even when all the world seems wrong,
to be someone's light is beautiful;
even when all hope seems gone.

@lyrically.blue

The Abyss

Trudging through the dark abyss of my mind, it is a scary thing that holds a lot of secrets that no one needs to know.

J.J.R
@the_poet_of_change

A Portion of Purpose

Make missions,
Go fishing,
Try eating something with nutrition.
Call yourself Christian, call yourself missing,
Anything at all,
Ride both the rise and the fall,
Horizon overriding, still deciding and surmising minutes while atoms are casually colliding.
Withdraw the assorted fortunes from the dormant shells that they dwell.
Call on your awesome, most of all, try your best -

Wish ya well.

Carlos Rodrigues

@IllestTraitor

Untitled

I have forgotten which day it is
I have forgotten who you are

But your face, it looks familiar
And I could tell

Your smile
Is just a farce

You asked me "how I was?"
As if I was a lost child

Waiting to be rescued.

But when you asked my name
I forgot or kept forgetting

"Who I was?"

Until it wiped my memory.. Clean

I am not sure it's quite right
How can I forget my name?

At this age, it gave me a fright

I could see them, standing
In front of me

Those familial faces
I barely recognised

They are feeling
Worried for me

How could I not know them?

When one of the girl's
Came up to me

And called me "Dad".

I felt a sharp pain
Piercing my heart

As I clenched my chest
And screamed, trying

To remember, so hard
Until I reached

My "Memory cues"
And I realised, who I was

A father, a husband and a son
With a duty to serve my family.

@viralvirus_official

Untitled

Sun warming and streaming on dreaming eyelids
squeezing, flutter, squinchy, blink.
The morning opens the book
and sleepily dip drips the ink.

The quill scribes with a scritch, scratch, swooshing.
The inky color bleeds brilliantly
over pressed paper pages smoothly.
My mind sends emotions bouncing
through confectionery sugared
cloudscapes abounding.

Diving head first into the illusionary,
eye spying the extraordinary,
fruitfully flowered prairie,
dreamily dazzled dew petalled through.

Excitedly drippy dipping the pen once more to
feel fanciful calligraphy swirl, dot, cross, curl and underscore.
My heart leaps from it's protective little cage and dances
freely across the page.

Like a gossamer winged fairy
dauntlessly dunking dainty toes
in the bright silvery estuary.

Numerous lovely landscapes with fantastical fairytale plots.
Drawings, poems and stories sought; sometimes even a quick witted thought.
Every morning, a fresh blank page,
then another when anxiety
finds the need to disengage.

Creating, calming, helping, healing
for the soul and for the mind.
Which ever imaginative task you choose in order to unwind,
do it fervently, unapologetically
and always be opine.

@dreadful_artist

Anxiety is Building

Anxiety is building
It's starting in my chest
My lungs constrict
Breath shallow but quick
I can feel the wave of dismay washing over me
My skin is buzzing while my hands are ready to dodge
Unwelcomed touches even if meant as a hug
These times I feel like hiding
These times I feel like crying
My tolerance is low and it's gonna show
Either I'll crumble or bite
I don't want to fight; with myself or with you
Whatever will we do

-Emily Salt
@emilysaltpoetry

Brightest Star

I see you
I know some people ignore you but
You deserve to be seen
You have a heart
You are a son, daughter, father, mother, friend
You are someone to somebody
You are someone to me
A love
A strength
A beauty so inner deep.
We all struggle
Sometimes we lose ourselves
But you my beautiful love
I want you back
Please let me help you
To find your way
For the world is missing it's brightest star

@invisibleme

Born in the Land of Earth

We are born to be happy in the land of Earth until episodes enter at its appointed time to experience dreadful feats.

I was born to experience short lived happiness until the time entered to spiral into the abyss of depression, anxiety, panic attacks, bipolar and post-traumatic stress disorder.

The very labels we put upon each other to give a name to the mental and emotional issues we encounter.

We are given pills in the attempt to control the behaviours, these insane mental sicknesses dictate as to how we will behave.

Yet, medications are but a temporary fix that inevitably cause more in depth symptoms of adverse reactions to the matter at hand we so desperately wish to abolish.

We believe what we are told and taught. These are just other experiences we are here to encounter.

We are born in the land of earth as experiencers to experience bittersweet encounters, which are merely lessons to learn by.

Living on a world of negative and positive forces are non-existent in Heaven. Only positive energy exists in the Kingdom of Heaven.

Negative energy is not permitted in Heaven. This is why illusional worlds were made to be born into so we can be given the opportunity to experience what we are not.

Christ tells us we receive what we ask. We asked to be born into a world where we can experience fear and darkness. However, in order for God to approve it, every soul had to be in agreement.

The moment we are born from out of timelessness into time, the memory of this is wiped out. This is the reason we ask the fundamental questions of blindness - why, what, where, when, how and are we alone.

Yet, we ask the very minds that do not know the answer. Pills do not deliver us from the mental state of mind that spirals us into its circle of gloom.

However, we are not forever doomed. It seems we are eternally lost, but we can be found.

State of mind can be restored to the vibrancy of who we truly are.

Through forgiveness is where I once again found happiness. I learned to forgive every individual and life episode, I believed was the cause to spiralling out of control and into the depths of insanity.

Through forgiveness, minds wellness prevailed. And kindness, humbleness, patience and peace followed. They are the spirit of love, light, life and truth. This is where insanity is restored to sanity. The essence of who we truly are.

At our willingness to forgive everyone and everything, we permit God to bless His divine miracles upon the crown of our head lifting us from the dead.

This is where I was delivered from all the medications that were prescribed to me as a temporary method to tweak my thinking to control behaviour. For it is how we think and what we believe that will dictate how we behave.

And so born in the land of earth, we are here to learn and remember to forgive one to another through every episode we encounter as experiencers. Through willingness to forgive, we overcome the insanity of mental illness and every dreadful experience. This is where we are divinely lifted into the realm of love, light, life and truth. The celestial forces we all seek while we are lost hoping to be found. Rest assure, at its appointed time, your miracle to deliverance from insanity is bound to enter. Restoration to minds wellness prevails under the veil of loves eternity, absolutely.

@godzillionloveandlight

This is Me

Hey. This is me,
What I choose to see,
What I believe.
Hey. This is me,
How I sing
And how I dream.
Hey. This is me,
No apologies
Reaching to my destiny.
Hey. This is me,
Scars and all
My beautiful flaws.
Hey! This is me,
How I dance
What I speak.
Hey! This is me,
My trials and struggles
Even my insecurities.
Hey! This is me,
All that I know
All that I do.
Hey! This is me,
What I have achieved
All my abilities.
HEY! This! is me,
How I walk
How I talk.
HEY! This! is me
The friends I make
The roads I take.
HEY! This! Is! me
Who I am inside
How I choose to shine
How I live
What I say
How I look.
HEY! THIS! IS! ME!
And there can be no other me because I'm already me
And I'm the best and only me there ever will be
And what I achieve is up to me
HEY! GUESS WHAT!
This is me
@miky_mike_

Untitled

The care for myself
Something I cannot neglect
My own sanity

The care for myself
This is not for anyone else
Only my own self growth

The care for myself
Forgiving past transgressions
My own sanity

The care for myself
Includes my mind body and soul
The whole piece of me

The care for myself
The path to my peace

@lindodapoet

Primal Fear

It tears the very flesh from me
up bubbles primal fight or flight.
Of frenzied manic symphony
from deep within a state of fright.
It reaps a heap of tangled veins
all tied together as a rope.
It blocks the calmness from my brain
to hang me dry when there's no hope.
All in my thoughts that try to see
beyond polluted waves of fear.
There's no one else around but me
so what does whisper in my ear.
That tells me all will eat my dreams
and spin my world into a dust.
Whilst split my mind right down its seams
to blow away in silent gust.

@poetry_viking

Freedom in Hope's Wings

I lay down in darkness again,
burrowed head in pillows,
soft blankets cause shivers
when wicked nightmares imprison
as they enter my dark purging realms,
whispering lies of my unworthiness,
awaiting my demise of forgotten deeds.
I remain in abject misery,
hopelessly a captive.
Grateful I'm supposed to be,
yet here I am sleepless, discontent
and unable to be concerned about others.
I smile and nod and say the right things
but no one realises I'm not there
I'm entrapped in the solitude of my mind.
When dawn approaches, I shut the windows to sleep
having stayed awake through the night
for fear of the shadows and shapes
evil makes on my wall.
Days pass into months
and then He came along,
springing back the curtains,
inviting that bright sun.
Laughter like a lost dream
I begin to hear,
uncertain at its beginning,
gasping on knowing its sound
had come from my lips so willingly.
For though the long winter was still
a part of my heart,
He'd brought hopeful spring
to sing songs to my soul.
-Freedom; Hope is a bird that sings as it flies
only when you give it its wings.

@reenadossauthor

Melancholy Ecstasy

(A 2 poet collaboration)

I feel the darkness bubble up inside, the moments of beautiful melancholy have taken a part of me that was once whole, shattered like a smashed mirror, my image is ripped away by my own mind. How could you do this to me? Leaving me intoxicated with darkness. Disassociated by my once magnificent self, unable to connect with this 'part of me'. You pierced my dreams and created nightmares, made me sing your mournful tune. Led me to believe I was nothing, the shadows dancing remind me of how lonely I am.
Here I go, split into all of the different scenarios, running and changing and crashing and waving-a signal, a sign, will anybody help me?
How confusing, I sound like I'm talking to someone else. A cold person causing this numbness inside of me to eat away at every beautiful cobweb. Yet, it isn't me I'm talking to. Is it?

by @baldilockswrites & @writingsofhairlocks

Life

Life can be cruel
Life can be tough
Life can be a bastard
When it gets too rough
Life can be wicked
Life can be mean
Life can be a heartbreaker
When you've seen what I've seen
But...
Life can surprise you
Life can be sweet
Life can be worthwhile
With good people you meet
Life can be tender
Life can be kind
Life can be beautiful
Just keep that in mind

@white_stag_poetry
Jesse Lee Staggs

Untitled

Everything is a lie, we all are liars
The world is unfaithful
What can we ever do to trust each other?
I wonder when it'll feel good to be myself again
Before I lost who I used to be
I'm walking in circles, with no direction ahead
Everything is colorful, yet everything is black
Nothing is ever good enough, yet it's all too much
I cry under my blankets wishing for goodness to stop and for me to finally find my old self again
I can never go back, I have to go forward
But how do you keep going forward
If all you know is circles?

@_darkness.within

Untitled

Cry not friend
Your garden will sing
Your dream symphony
Beneath the blue moon
And smooth the ache
With music.

@asta_lander

Untitled

One day you'll look back
At how everything has changed
How everything brings peace
Your mind's off the stress
But till then
You can grieve the loss
Its no shame to welcome the pain
And feel it coursing throughout your chest
You can cry away the hurt
Or turn it into art
You can lay all day in bed
Or put your pain into rhymes
You can show the world
You are not okay
Because it takes strength to
Not hide your real self
And admit
That I am not okay
Its fine if you are not doing fine
If you can't get up from your bed
If you can't go out with your friends
If you have lost the love of your passions
If you have no faith but you are breathing
With time things will change
And you'll find that hope again
Till then just breathe
And let yourself be
Because one day you'll look back
At how everything has changed
And you are doing better
Than you would have imagined

@adee.writes

Never Stop Being You

Never let others' negativity dull your light.
Remember that your star will shine forever bright.
Let those who you love guide you along the way.
No matter where life takes you, in their heart you'll stay.
Never think for a moment that you're not any good,
Or that anyone will replace you; no one ever could
Know that people truly appreciate what you do
And most importantly, never stop being you.

@jen.elvy_poems

More Than a Bad Day

I'm not crazy or insane,
But this is a little more than just a bad day.
Give me a moment
and let me explain..

You live your life,
Mines the same.
You have sunny days,
I get flooding rain.
You have happy thoughts,
Mine are black and grey.
Your life is fun,
Yet mines a drain.
You laugh out loud,
And I cry in shame.
You say nothing,
While I'll complain.
You can do no wrong,
While I get all the blame.
My mind may be weak,
But I'm not insane.

@the_illiterate_poet70

Inner Voice

Too long, have I sat awaiting, bursting with such an agitation growing in your subjugation,

Too weak I have been in my faltering seemingly redundant retaliation.

Within you I have watched you, sat perched adjacent,
Whilst you just disregarded me so blatant,
With growing discord increasingly complacent.

Have you not heard me call you?
Shouting out your name?
Have you not seen the messages I've left for you?

So clear have I tried to help you,
So many signs in my attempts to reign, in your thoughts, your actions, all of your foolish deeds,
Each time it hasn't changed a thing, nothing that I ever do succeeds.

I've been doing a lot of thinking,
whilst you've ignored me,
my influences shrinking,
But I've heard and seen enough now and it's time for you to hear me!
Hear me, heed me whilst more than ever now you need me.

I haven't sat away hidden, shrunk, defeated,
all my will unbidden,

I've been resting,
growing stronger!
Planning, investing,
in re-acquainting
my efforts with you,
For you can't go on like this no longer!

No more can this continue to go on
unchecked, unpunished,

Unburden yourself once and for all!
Don't ignore me a second longer,
together we'll walk openly and tall,

Relinquished of the demons whispers
that grew louder since you were small.
You have it in you
to make it through

if only, please!
You would just listen,

To me again I'll guide you along,
we'll make those eyes again
dance, sparkle, glisten.

Together you and I, we'll make it better from now on.

We can't undo all what you've done,
that's the past let us leave it gone.

Just listen to me and I'll tell you what I've learned,
In my pensive cell sat seething with you.

As with each denial of me you hurt and burned.
But broken you have never made me,
scarred and yes betrayed,
Yet I forgive you as you hear me now, no
longer am I mislaid.

It is the time for you,
to break on through,
that wall of all your
many bricks,
No more games,
no more reckless disregard,
no more hiding
behind an easy fix!

You're not meant to be the
way you've been,
how people know you from
what they've seen.

Return again just how you
truly are, gentle, honest, caring.

Instead of shrugging off what you will not face,
Shrug off the bitter heartless mask you're wearing.

You care so much yet you carry on you fool!
Too scared to stand and fight,

Like a coward you simply go on and hide,
Every time just choosing flight.

Stand up and be a man young boy!
Act your age you're simply a disgrace!

Going around acting how you have,
with such a wake, a mess left in each place.

I know you don't intend, indeed you don't set
out to hurt how you have done,
But you've got to stop what you are doing, now!
Let this be a new day that's begun. . . .

Begin to listen, to listen to
me and act upon my words.

I am you,
your conscience,
your heart and soul,

The voice of loved ones
torn apart,
Asking please now make
this your last fresh start,
Make things better, finally,
as a whole.

People can only truly
forgive you when you
truly start the change,

There's still time for you
to put things right,
to slowly rearrange,

Make ever lasting
amends, now mean it,
Believe it and your
heart will cleanse,
your soul begin to really
feel it.

Trust in me I'll help you find peace once more.
And one last final time
I will now again implore.

You listen to me
for goodness sake with your

ears open wide!

We have begun now
and with time it will show,
will tell,
As you slowly lift,
from now on to keep,
your head raised up with pride.

@scarlarjpoetic

Chasing Tranquillity

Quiet seas
hiding verdigris
hands of mine
hold lightening skies
yellow poppies
dress my lies
fake smiles
breathe in hope
tempers flare
between
sunlight and shadows
amorous heart
pierced with love
doomed forever
in boketto
past beginnings
of a broken rainbow
tactile grief
masked in lilac skies
it's a beautiful mind
collecting dust
echoes from the future
wakes serpentine dreams
midnight maddening no more
bitter betrayals
be my lungs
Remember!
Remember now!
Anchor!
Anchor strong!
buzzing bees, stop your songs
monarchy of anarchy
Ends now!
path is clear
from this quatervois
Copper rings
my scattered mind
Focus head!
Focus now!
Jump thou not
From here to there
Forgo your impulse
Channel peace

Don't lose me, yet again
To a mere kiss of fate.

Janani @pennyformythoughts_

Untitled

It's okay to struggle
and cry a better tomorrow,
is only a day away.

@poemsbystephanie1

Untitled

It never hits you until it's too late, when you're existing solely from a mattress and your skin has become sweatpants. Your head is growing more grease than hair, and your teeth are chronically fuzzy. At first you couldn't stop eating, but now you can't even remember whether or not you've had breakfast. Cooking requires moving, and moving requires energy. Which is now your body's rarest resource.

The worst part is the way it lies to you. The way it seeps through the cracks of your thoughts and turns them dark, turns them sharp. Just a head full of jagged edges, and a mind set to self destruct. For a while you hated how everything would make you cry, but now you wish you could go back to those days of bursting at the seams. You thought feeling sad all the time was such a nightmare, but now you realize that feeling nothing is worse. Much worse.
Because if you can't feel, are you still living? Have you been existing as a ghost?
I think that might be the perfect way to describe "living" with depression... Existing as a ghost. A ghost of the person you used to be. A shell you barely recognize unless you squint.

It never hits you until it's too late, that seemingly unavoidable rock bottom, but sometimes it takes one giant smack to send a jolt through your body. To your heart. To your mind. In order for life to begin existing again beneath your skin.

@themusingsofmollymaven

The Last Reminder

"You are so good, who are you dear?"

Awhile she muttered, my tears spilled,
Careening down the face, unwilled,
A wave astounding ran across,
Obscured of my impending loss.

A wizened weather beaten soul,
Distinguished woman as a whole,
Destroyed the fort of memory,
By an amnesiac misery.

The fight with delusional phantasm,
Enduring painful muscle spasm,
Indrawn, aphasia, worsen,
In an Alzheimer battling person.

Dismayed descry, my mother's plight,
Restriction and care braced her fight,
With humor, music, I distract,
Routine makes positive impact.

Albeit declension rate is norm,
Remained a friend in mighty storm,
Psychosis of Alzheimer's patient,
Could reduce the risk with education.

@harvestingmind

Stronger

I take strength from my fake smiles
The ones I give out when I want to hide
My pain, my hurt, my frown, it's only just a little lie
Still my fake smiles delivers me through the last mile

I take strength from the gratitude I feel in my heart
You may not deserve it, but it is still a part
Of this parcel I call my emotional spectrum
I still wake up and thank you, I take this gratitude and make it my chosen art

I take strength from my memories of you
You inspired me, then broke me, but still the memories stayed true
That I can look past the greens and the reds and not remain blue
I stand here stronger, darling, stronger than the damsel you didn't rescue!

I take strength from my Today
As I watch my Todays become Yesterdays
I know I will make it through this day
To live another Tomorrow, as it becomes my Today

-Anu CN
@allyouneedisalilbitofsugar

Untitled

my wrist was once a canvass of all my unwanted artworks
an excuse to wear long sleeves during summer
a physical manifestation of the noise in my head and the whimper escaping my mouth

my wrist was once a capsule of all my insecurities
thinking that maybe if I pile them all in one area, it won't escape to other parts of my body
like a mirror, only it deflects

my wrist was once a whore for sharp objects
she fucked them despite the presence of the sun during midday
believing she found love in those moments

now my wrist turned her battle cries into songs,
permanent tattoos patenting the person I've become

each translucent line creating a path towards my future
now my wrist is a museum, a history book, a mother

@ollivernylpoetry

Perspective

Everyday I sat by the darkness
It seemed so perfect
Flawlessly hiding my scars
And my weakness that ate me
As self-love came late to me
It took time
To love how flawed
And yet, a beautiful soul I held
Depression gave loneliness
And scars for life
While the self-love I allowed in,
Gave me peace
From the inside
And my flaws
Felt inferior
The fear of not being loved
Felt extreme
But those flaws,
When I loved them for self
When they were just me
And not my flaws anymore,
I raised past them
To not erase those
Or to be loved by everyone
But to accept them,
Improve them
And to love myself
Over everyone

@sana_poet

Criminal Minds

Residing in the confines of my mind,
lies the crimes of times I wish to rewind,
where memories exists from a smog made abyss,
that persist in the mist of a deadly cyst.

"How will I ever peak if my thoughts are this weak,
mirroring the faults I display every week."

There are the too many meetings,
where I'm often left screaming,
a painful beating of reflective memories,
that deepen the effects of my tragedies,
where trauma grows and I'm despised,
by my own mind telling me criminal lies,
so I look to stride & ride back to my tide,
hoping I'll be able to stand high with my pride.

@epilepsy_in_motion

Untitled

I know it feels like
someone turned the lights off
And you're stumbling around
in unending darkness

But trust me when I say
One day the switch will flip
It takes but an instant
for light to breach dark

Until then, darling,
When the demons come calling
Let them meet that girl
who sings yesterday
so sweetly in the today

Loving hands will catch
should you fall
Loving hearts will hear
when you call

@poetscapes

Metamorphosis

I could tell you a million stories
Of lost dreams left in the clouds
Tiny scars kissed by the stars
And of times I have not been proud
Footprints left to wash away
A wild souls loss of hope
Danger found beneath the ground
Embracing the slippery slope
But we all have many moments
When the daffodils die inside
And the lilac rivers no longer flow
Because all of our tears have dried
And have you seen me lately?
Hiding within my cocoon?
The change is slow and painful
Butterfly wings don't grow too soon
But if patience is a virtue
I will wait another day
For if sweet peace provides release
It is here I need to stay

By Kelly Goudreau
@poeticpiper

Untitled

Be one with your inner core
Inside you, find strength
Don't doubt your frail voice from within
Telling you to focus your heart's mind
Shut those exhausted eyes and take a tiny break from life, so called reality and the imposed truth.
Just be you
Feel the pearls of existence, the wind is blowing on your face
Because you are glorious
And people will always try to pull you down by reacting,
So just act on your dreams, your passion, your responsibilities
Keep up your discernible actions
And go on
Ahead..
Shining..

@wordeliciouspoetry

Falling Blinds

There is sunshine in
this rainstorm. If there wasn't, love,
we couldn't see the rain.

@17_syllables_poetry
Aurora Turkenburg

Forgiveness

One day I will accept my own forgiveness
for every time I turned love away
for fear of breaking too much
for fear of what people would think
if I unravelled in front of them
for fear of the mess I would become
if I allowed my inside to be my outside
for believing my composure was evidence of my recovery
when my mess is soil from
which healing grows

@susurruspoetry

The Guest

It is here
The uninvited guest
A shadow of comforting sorrows
Like a blanket upon shoulders
dropping upon one at will
with a sweet lull into despaired inertia
I do not know its origin or end
But it is here
Again

@julieonohwrites

Thank Your Memories

Get rid of a memory, you can't forget
How hard you try, but your mind just won't let
You leave the past where it belongs
Reminded by some smells and songs
They take you back to that same place
You see so clearly now their face
So many, many big mistakes
Your head was not in the right place
And things you wish you'd never felt
Or done, or been, it can't be helped
Goodbye, so long, please leave me be
I want to lose this memory
But places deep within your mind
Know better than to leave behind
A part of life that meant so much
Even if the nature their was such
That it left you healing, don't feel whole
But life goes on, and know your soul
Does not get healed by hiding the past
Instead move on, and feel at last
A heavy weight gone from your heart
For the first time in years you start
To live your life, the here and now
And thank your memories, they showed you how

Taylor Tippins
@geminiandthewolf

The Language of Silence

How do you free your tongue
From society's chains
Of honour and submission
How do you heal rotting wounds
When the same people who hold the cure
chose to stab you.
How many long sleeve shirts do you wear
To hide those chiselled wrists and
How many cuts does it take to release the agony .

I want to know,

How many boys does it take to destroy one girl
And how many girls can together destroy years of friendship,
How do you react when you cross paths 5 years later
And he still grins to remind you how he mercilessly victimised that 12 year old girl.

Tell me my love,

How many boxes of hope
Can you fill
With those empty, broken promises
And
How many anxieties do you run from
When they live and breathe
In your mind and
eat the flesh off your thoughts.
How many tears
Do you wipe
From your own eyes until
Your eyes turn into numb
Lifeless pits of misery.
How many times do you weep
When you see mothers and daughters hand in hand both deeply in love.
How do you cope with the jealousy when you see mothers fight for their daughters rights.
How many years of hard work will it take to hear the words you've craved to hear all your damn life;
'I'm proud of you my daughter'
When do you stop searching for validation in Daddy's eyes and accept that you can never be what he has envisioned.
You are not the son he wanted.
You are not his pride.

How many mirrors do you speak to

Until you accept that none are listening.
How many dreams do you grasp onto
When they tear each one ruthlessly from your tiny hands?
How many ambitions do you fight for
Until they coerce your tender voice
Into eternal suffocation.
How many times do you cry to the heavens for respite and how do you ask God for mercy.
How many dusks do you sit and count before you wait for the sun to rise on your land .

And,

When night casts its peripheral shadows
Where do you hide -under blankets or behind cabinets of pills.

How do you deal with 3am flashbacks that cease time
and why do you sleep - to escape life or escape tiredness.

Tell me,

How many candles do you light
In your quest for vision
And for how long do you exist
Before you start living ?

But more importantly,

how
Do you scream and yell
and plead
For people
To understand why
You were quiet
All this time
How do you make them
understand why you write .

I want to know ,

How do you speak
In the language of silence and still be heard?

- internal struggle

@aiyesha__

An Exercise in Being Honest with my Monsters

who?
the ghosts of past me's whispering into the ear of present me so that future me might have a chance to heal.

how?
I picked up a pen and held it to the paper to see if my thoughts would bleed.

why?
it was safer than lighting a match against my skin to turn the trauma into ash

where?
in beige panelled rooms with a chair that squeaked and a condescending tone that brought out the fire in me

when?
in between moments of falling helplessly down rabbit holes of memories and resurfacing just long enough to catch my breath, ever trying to escape me

remember?
yes, I do.

—z.z

@writingpoemsinthedark

Ombre Stories

I know of a midnight blue adorned in shards of grey
and of bleeding red soaking worn canvasses,
that rise from their stupor on the infernal bay
and drink from my soul to build carcasses.

These netherworld beings dangle on the last thread of hope,
catching me unawares on the sidewalk even on bright, sunny days
fickle and cruel, they huddle together on a dangerous tightrope
choking me to death in a hundred devious ways.

They drag me into the dank black hole of grief
and drown me in swamps of looming defeat,
holding hostage my limp body they carve their commands on the fief,
my new gangster friends are too insistent to be snubbed on the street.

But there will come a day I step into the glow of the morning sun,
dragging feet and soul and hope as heavy as lead
to stumble upon a sanguine lullaby, hushed and outdone,
yet awaiting my departure from the House of the Dead.

Daisies and orchids will replace the thorns
that now lay scattered and unperturbed in my backyard,
I will breathe the scent of tomorrow on a dewy morn
and paint a star for every jagged shard.

I will write of the still wintry nights, lit irradiant by the hearthside, and
of monsters roaring in the dark, yet caged in my words,
I will kiss gentle hands in a sea of stench, lest they chide
my impotence, and condemn me to the thunderbirds.

Truth be told, there are only tales spawned off day and night
where black and white doggedly walk astride,
free to blend in a kaleidoscope of the mind's eye,
or weave sagas where melancholy hides.

Someday I will choose a midnight blue pierced by the cries of a mockingjay
await my turn on the precipice of time, like the strongest of the mulberry trees,
steal a glorious feather or two from the old phoenix gone astray,
and birth a dulcet tune along the frayed edges of my ombre stories.

@julyblossom23

My Phone Lights up in the Shotgun Seat

my phone lights up in the shotgun seat like a bullet / again / my foot pushes harder on the accelerator / I send my dad to voicemail / again / there's something funny about my front right tire / but I can't stop / drive drive drive / the steering wheel quakes in my hands / I send my mom to voicemail / send my sisters to voicemail / send my brothers to voicemail / send you to voicemail / finally turn off my phone / throw it onto the floor of the back seat / let it explode while I scream-sing to ridiculous, wonderful pop songs / drum my shaking hands on the steering wheel / change the station when commercials come on / forget rear-view mirrors exist / watch the sunrise from my car / stop only for coffee or gas / forget I'm not the only person in the world

everything blurs when i drive past & I'm everywhere & nowhere all at once

—mary e

@maryewrites

Off the Ledge

There are days when the lungs are so good at their job, you don't even notice
their rise and fall, the oxygen swirling.
And then there are days where breathing feels like you've got a hundred-pound boulder
pressing down on your chest.
You're too aware of it—you try to breathe deep but can't.
These are the days when the eyes are an ocean, limbs are lead,
the heart is nothing more than an organ.
These are the days that the darkness will try to win you over
with empty promises you'll be so desperate to believe
that you'll swallow them whole.
But happiness doesn't come from the bottom of a pill bottle,
tip of a knife, end of the gun barrel—
only death.
And I know you know that.
I know that's what you are so desperate for.
I know that you'd crawl on bare belly to scrape the numbness out of your legs,
to taste blood in your mouth.
And I know you won't believe me when I say that everything
is temporary—but
everything
is
temporary.
If you don't believe me, turn your face up toward the sun.
Each night it dips below horizon.
Has the sun never turned back up come morning?
Have the moon and stars ever stopped offering light in the meantime?
Look at the seasons, the rise and fall of the tides.
If the Earth teaches us anything, it's that nothing is permanent.
Some seasons may last months, others can stretch for decades.
But eventually the leaves begin their return to Earth;
eventually life freezes over;
eventually, like clockwork, the snow melts and seeds blossom.
You can still slingshot back from the edge of the abyss,
reach for these outstretched words instead:
I know that Winter can feel like the end of things,
but there are so many flowers that have yet to bloom
and so many sunrises ahead.

@kaitquinnpoetry

Untitled

i.

she's transparency of light
crawling, sunglow arteries
and mosaic butterflies
in the rose garden curve

of her hips, vertebrae
sprouting dead leaves
knots in her anatomy
a songbird of sin;

she sings of devoured blasphemy,
hallowed out in glorious fire,
radiating—her anvil rings
of thunder and war;

star-peppered eyes
cast in acrimony; these origami dreams
strung between chalk veins
and dry rot bones, too deep.

ii.

she is: copper lips, citrus kiss,
flesh made of storms,
a crucifix on her tongue,
religion swallowed thickly;

her lavender soul a beautiful mess
overrun by hungry wolves
flashing their teeth and loving
with a twist of blue nightmares.

her spine's seeping, freezing
numb smiles seeking warmth
on whiskey tongues
and pharmaceutic wonders

whilst pretty boys decipher the atlas
of her thighs, the fireflies
alight in her salted lungs
reaching for empty galaxies.

iii.

she felt eternal: immortalised
between heartbeats and bedsheets
black teeth bleeding ichor,
a taste of wanderlust

and she rises like a wave
her nakedness brilliant sunshine,
golden starlight mired in feverish bones,
guarded by nothing

but proud shoulders.
healing heart made of moondust
and kindred echoes of the sea
on bare skin, marred skin

unbending, wild beast
see the flash of mischief
of being too much to hold and—

oh darling,

don't you give them an inch.
@arotuy

Mushroom Clouding

you curl up silent next to me in a bed too small in which to be lonely
breath heavier than lead administered in passages of my china soul
I offer paper-bagged prayers to the ceiling from underneath your seatbelt arm
a spider tightropes down from it's corner seeking out a sole ember of you
and wanders towards an untouched foothold on my rock-wall free climbed by your scorn

my salt-lake lips crack under the effort to move apart
the sound of me disappears in tremors of my lifeblood
I fall deep into the well of your casketing silence
it vampires at the empty bricks that clog up my throat

I purchase delicate words and peg them on the lifeline strung between us
imploring the stone-throwing storm in tongues I cannot twist to make my own
so you don't lean too far off the hungry cliffhangers wagering your fall
lies you trapped are waiting to roll down the slope of your sorrow-hewed truth
but you tall-tell a toy soldier's return from war with your bullet-proof ghost

your blackest blood boils inside your room
as moth-winged murmurs membrane the night
I breathe it in too: the grimy ache
seeping in through my ventilation
smoking my sleep with jump-start nightmares
of wool-pulled days when we pocketed
each other's all-consuming pulse

the drumrolls sounding a half beat out of time
a fractured bone that has never been set right

carpeted over by *never fit in* crime
but nothing could anchor to the us that fought
off vultures and selves in our butterfly gloves

and of all the wants you wanted most
with the darkness hounding at your feet
the silt of us was the first you lost
when you hurled us to the dark to feed
@widwords

My Way Back Home

An open book,
My pages lay torn and crumpled around the office of my therapist.

We've spent nearly an hour debating metaphysics
and family visits,
Flaws, the vice of addicts and the virtue of abusive
Brush strokes striking my canvas.

Until it's time to wait for the next appointment.
And I'll shed a storm before
she hears my song,
Always ending with an
Anacrusis.

An arbitrary journey home feels like an odyssey,
Drained of all zeal,
Never armour nor ardour to carry,
benumbed body back from sea to shore.

Thankfully there's a bus,
but it grinds and stumbles against riotous roads.
The city alive with challenging enthusiasm.
My reality survives on rotating exhaustion.

I'm back so I breathe again,
I can lay my resolve naked on the bed
With gusto and imagined gravitas,
My anxiety no longer at critical mass.

In a sense,
I've made my way back home.
In another,
There's no quarter.
Until I learn a love that's out of reach,
And then one day I'll cure my loneliness.
@kurtedwardspoetry

Untitled

It comes for me.
Sits on my chest.
Squeezes my throat.
Chokes me.
Surrounds me
in it's tangled web.
Enters me.
Fills me with dread.
Wave after wave
the darkness comes.
Crashing into me.
Breaking me down
'til I'm begging
to drown.

©J.E.Spradlin
@jesthepoet

Dear You

I know you are hurting
That weight on your shoulders
Slowly burying you to your own grave

It whispers lies to you; I know that
It poisons your heart until all you bleed is dark matter; I know you're hurting

This is a letter to you little one
The fire in your bloodstream, You
Sky high dreams, You

A reminder that if you're reading this letter, rejoice for you've made it this far

I am writing to You
To tell you that I know for I was there too but now I am here
For every tempest is followed by a rainbow

Sincerely Me, who used to suffer greatly

@_kimenyembo_

Not for the Naked Eye

You don't see it when you look at me
It's not visible for the naked eye to see
It's inside my brain
It's not what they call physical pain
It's going from zero to a hundred in a second
It's the classic of don't touch the red button
That's my anxiety
And it's part of me
It's not being able to breathe
It's being afraid everyone will leave
When they find out what I try to hide
It's an extra person next to my side
Whispering toxic thoughts in my ear
Are you still here?
I can't see you
I can't hear you
It's overwhelming

@poetessofhearts

Rise in the East

When the sky seems dark
As the lights go dim
You might have lost your spark
And have nowhere to begin

When you look up just to see
These scary dark clouds
And the thunders of your fear
Are shouting up loud

Just have a look around
See, you are not alone
As the cold winds are flowing
Just to make you breath in this zone

Have some faith
the way you climb up with a rope
As you have a light inside
With a never dying hope

You might be feeling tired
You might be fallen too
But there's a long way, Go!
No one can dare stop you!

You know, you're born to fly...
You're born to fight, oh beast...
You are the Sun, you know?
You've got to rise in the East..

©Shubhankar Bhagwat @words_on_the_wheels

Real Face

Nobody ever asked why I wear makeup,
A little bit, but still enough to notice,
Maybe they think it's a perfect way to hide my face,
Insecurities and imperfections,
Unaware of my chaotic world,
Or maybe they think it's the way I please others,
Undesired and unreal,
But what they don't know is reality,
What they don't see is misery,
I conceal my under eyes,
To hide the dark circles after I've been on a spree of sleepless nights,
I use eyeliner,
Just to define my eyes a bit,
After they've shed all the tears,
Or tried to hold them inside,
I do it so I only notice the line,
Not my puffy eyes,
I use highlight to make my face slight shiny,
Making illusion,
After I've almost forgot to smile,
What they see and what I feel,
There's deep gap between,
I don't wear it with pride,
To me it's just a choice,
Even if I don't sometimes,
They say I don't look alike,
All girly and endearing,
They don't notice my invisible smile,
As it never was a thing,
As it doesn't exist.

@poetrybydolly

Facets of Myself

Like different colors of a prism glinting in the sun,
a full spectrum of emotions shape my inner dialogue.
Most often a running diatribe;
commentary about my shortcomings, mistakes and faults.
The clear glass foundation upon which my fragile ego teeters precariously;
a pole dancer twirling on an invisible filament between the window frame and the hanging pendant.
But if it spins just right,
the sunlight finds a different facet;
refracting to illuminate an alternate version of myself.
A burst of bright yellow joy.
Vibrant blue rivers of creativity.
A magnificent magenta splash of deeply rooted strength.
The world sees mostly clear glass with clean edges, precise lines, and smooth faces;
a solid figure.
Yet still,
in private moments of abject beauty...
color leaps out onto a wall,
falls upon the floor,
Or crawls across the ceiling;
too bright to contain.
A fleeting rainbow of my best self.

@wheelacw32

Constant Weather in Changing Seasons

The clouds have come
in the middle of spring.
I hear the sound of rain
approaching - a definite falling,
no ambivalent gestures this time.
there only is
the throbbing pain,
where once a nest was made,
for Life to thrive.
Confusion overwhelms my mind
and
takes out the little left of my time.
Is it easier to mourn
a certainty that you perceive?
Or does the uncertain spark
warm the cold of your insides?
I do not know of seasons and their meanings,
All I know
is a rain that's coming,
All I feel
is a constant weather breathing.
@chrevitch

Hummingbird

I'm restless.
Mind empty, noiseless.
This silence is deafening.
My body thrums, desperate to move,
and yet, directionless,
I've run out of reasons to.
I'm a hummingbird.
Carrying the weight of my own cage
upon my wings.
One day, perhaps,
I'll leave these bars behind,
dropped from great heights
into the ocean,
alongside the last of my tears.
For all these years I've hovered, desperately searching for more.
But on that day,
on that day,
finally,
my heart will soar.

@bodiposipoet

Red Hibiscus

A small red flower stood by my side, when I was alone and there was no light. It could whisper to my inner turmoil soothed the caresses of my heart. It let me see a speck of light when all else was dark.

Neha Taneja
@neha.m.taneja

A Note to Anxiety

Dear anxiety,
My mind is clean, free, and pure.
It is filled with light.
It is filled with love.
It is filled with peace.

Dear anxiety,
My mind is clean, free, and pure.
It holds no space for you.
It holds no space for you.

Dear anxiety,
This is where we take different paths
that leads to different directions.
Bye for LIFE.

@yelewrites

Depression is Real

My name is depression and I have a few confessions. My mind runs on a lot of tension that sometime drives me in a different direction. At times I need to a little extra attention because of a simple rejection. Other times it's because I hate my not so perfect reflection. I require a lot more comprehension. Treat me with compassion and you might see a blossoming transformation.

@the_sparrowstories

In The Dark

In the dark I stand all alone,
In the dark that I for sure, know is my home;
I think of hope in the dark,
I think of the faintest possibilities in the dark,
In the dark!

Someone lead me to the light,
Oh! Come on, end my plight;
Give me a reason to rejoice in delight,
Delight!

So here I am in the dark,
As I await,
In the dark,
Standing all alone,
Alone!

For every tear I shed, life takes away a piece of the night;
With every piece of false light, faith owns my soul,
I love it, but will life ever return my peace?

In the dark I stand,
I stand all alone.
Even the heart can not keep me away,
I still fight to keep the blood in my veins.

Sukanya Basu Mallik

@sukanyabasumallik_official

My Truth...

I felt the need to cry today,
to let me heart speak it's truth.
I'm usually so reserved,
that it never really gets to.
So, I let it go. Let it all release.
I guess I didn't realize how bad I was truly hurting.
And I know my heart is so full. So full of lovely things.
But there are so many times when it gets so lonely.
My heart has so much to give and it only asks one thing; It just wants to be enough for someone. It needs love to set it free.

@amoriepoetry

Collaboration

(7 Poet Collaboration)

Bipolar seeming trapped in solar dark,
extremisms spark this psycho clash within,
then losing source of light as I remark;
whilst sitting with my evil twin... can't win.

An overpowering voice tells me I'm alone.
It feels as if my life just isn't my own.
With every pretend smile leaving an inner cyclone
And an icy chill in each and every bone.

My eyes keep drifting into distant dreams
as flies and ants relate their fairy tales
and conversations lead to stifled screams;
All tendencies to numb this go off-rails.

Ideas and thoughts in my head I desire,
To express, yet the knots together chain
Can not protest with my stomach in wires,
I know this is a cage, but in these strains
I feel secure, unsure if it's mistrust
But I feel help isn't needed with this pain

Endured attacks of panic I can't bear,
all while I'm choking by my breath, I fear,
that still there's nothing known and nothing's clear.
I live my life accompanied by fear,
not fair? Then still I find none really cares!
She talks in jibbers this once bubbly gal,
as brain games form a beautiful betrayal
and checkmate this girl harshly as she goes,
Anxiety remains her friendly foe,
her lips are sewn, but echoes of her mind
are tired of this constant verbal grind.
These spinning, fainting, also fatal thoughts;
and so depression, hail to you! She lost.

But would she give up simply just like that,
would she despair the life that she begat,
This once, whose aura did each one inspire.
That one, who filled their every heart's desire
But how could she succumb to all this pain
and why would she choose life filled with disdain?
It's time she rose above this morbid fear

and step out of her darkened, woeful sphere.

@butchkassedy,

@the.shades_sarah.writes

@niels_schoenmaker

@miky__mike__

@wordsdepth

@confessions_of_sophia

@harvestingmind

Anatomy of OCD

Every tilt, every slit; all little bits
bother me such, I can't ever perch.

Your dot perturbs me, so do the crooked lies;
eat me up alive.

I can't deal with an infinitesimal slight, without plight; although a trite, someday my
might will sun the sight on the jagged height of a nebula breathing out of a soul slowly
singed, a pulsating mind, a wandering heart—- rivulets of rhyme on this starry night.
I wash my hands, round and round, a hundred spikes itching the skin; pert to ragged in
a futile attempt to never touch what has been fingerprinted.

The ooze controls the fall of an eternal waterfall hindering my mania.

@essentiallydonut

Glass Girl

Chapter 1

Girl of glass has a heart that beats so softly it doesn't make a sound
She swells with each breath but becomes more fragile
She swallows her feelings and they slip into the hollow shell of her
Girl of glass stands still in a crowded room, too easy to break to risk moving
She stares with doll eyes watching as people look right through her
She feels full of emptiness and shatters
Girl of glass is swept under the rug
She has no worth if she can't hold things
She is too many sharp pieces to risk stepping on

Chapter 2

Her mind jagged shards with sharp tongue
Her body a one way mirror
She sees out and no one sees in
Twisted thoughts carving deep cracks
Lining them with gold only makes her more beautiful
That's why...
They love her so much more broken.
Breaths as fragile as blown glass
Heavy heart beats in a hollow chest
Sadness echoes in her

@ajblueorion

Stolen

You meet him, you love him, you give up your life,
of cocktails and clubbing to become his wife.
You try for a baby and when you conceive,
your job is the next thing that you have to leave.
Life with a new born can be quite a bind,
before very long away goes your mind.
It's all about baby and you feel ignored,
daytime TV leaves you stupid and bored.
There's the odd coffee morning or 'Ladies Lunch' maybe,
but the No.1 topic will always be Baby.
As your bundle gets bigger and looks less like Shrek,
fatigue and time famine mean that you look a wreck.

When hubby comes home he sprints through the muddle,
his sole aim and mission: to give baby a cuddle.
Each day is a tunnel, through which you must lurch,
the old you is missing- but there isn't a search.
They say motherhood helps a woman to grow,
it's true of your body, but not your mind though.
I must say that babies bring joy beyond measure,
But the bit that they steal, is a bit that you treasure.

@rhymes_n_roses
Sharron Green

Morning Comes

Morning comes,

It always does.

Yet countless nights you told yourself

you'd never make it through,

And you believed the dawn would come

for everyone but you.

Through endless nights your heart would bleed

for what it could not do,

Still you would beg it to go on

though you were bleeding too.

The nights your weary soul would cry

for daggers that life threw,

And found the child who hides inside,

the one who no one knew.

The child who carries all the scars

from violent storms that blew,

And bears the pain of loneliness

from love that wrath withdrew.

So, reach for her and take her hand,

the time is overdue,

To dry the tears that she still cries;

the tears that fall for two.

Then, gently take her in your arms,

for trust she must renew,

And give her shelter, keep her safe,

that child, you see, is you.
And when you give that little girl
the love that she is due,
Then all the nights you told yourself
you'd never make it through,
The nights your aching heart would bleed
for what it could not do,
And nights your weary soul would cry
for daggers that life threw,
Will plague you naught, will evanesce,
and you will find it true...
Morning comes,
It always does.

@midnightmusings_rt

Stronger

Teased.
Made fun of, when there is nothing funny about me.

Picked on, laughed at.
Everyone laughing,
but me.

Surrounded.
Trapped by the stares, the snickers.
The haters, the whispers.

Everyday, their words bang against my head,
Trying to get into my brain,
but I won't let it.
The tears burn my face at night, cause I can't forget it.
I perspire, my body cries, but I try not to sweat it.

Stop with the HATE,
the obsession over weight,
whether one is gay or straight,
so what, I may be shy,
I am smart, not a geek
Just cuz I am not wearing Jordan's, I must meet my defeat?
If I have a disorder, or a different skin color...
Don't you sit there & judge me, cuz this here is out of order...

Stop with the HATE
Yes, I practice a different religion, or I am from a foreign place,
Don't criticize, open your eyes, you may find your faith,
I may have an accent, or dress differently,
Don't you dare point those fingers at me.

I am not here to be judged by you
Before you go throwing in your two cents, Remember your currency makes no sense.
Your words are worthless. I am not con-tent; your bullying is nonsense, that I will not accept.

Because I am stronger.

It's time for me to stand up,
Change my life for the better
Positively, with help, I will make my life better.

Because I am stronger.

© Jereni-Sol
@jerenisolpoetry

Untitled

Words are shut in my throat
Tears got dried
I'm totally lost
When to laugh
When to cry
I couldn't learn to act
and react
Like others do
Does it mean they all are normal
and I'm abnormal, is it true
Isn't it that normal is an abstract term
Defined in terms of majority
And not in terms of morality
or humanity
And if I'm not acting like majority
Why it can't be
That I'm the only normal among so many abnormal
And why to get declared as normal
I have to kill my spontaneity?

@theworldthroughmyeyes2015

POP

I bottle up my stress till
I can shake it just slightly
and turn the cork into a lethal weapon
POP: you're dead, I'm spent—
my contents spilled,
the place is trashed, and I think

Damn, that peace was expensive.
Now it's all over the floor.

@eliseemersynpoetry

Void. Flower

Somewhere in all this
There exists
Something blooming
Radiant against the backdrop
Of the cold endless abyss
It's pedals never wilting
Forever open to the void

It soaks in the darkness
And blooms further still
A peculiar sight
Roots of intrigue
Twist and turn
As they propagate
Through nothing at all.

It is so beautiful
Yet so lonely
To pick such a thing
Would be to remove it
from this world
A mutually appealing prospect
However this can not be so
It's essence must remain
Intact.

You see,
If not for this flower
This realm would truly be
Empty.

@void_vis_vires

Self Appraisal

I think it's really me
that needs reminding
how awesome I am.
No one else.
I am pretty fucking awesome!
Listen self!

JMK
@amusemeamuseisme

Dear Mind of Mine

How I wish you and I had a better relationship...
Your love really is the only love that would fulfil the yearning in my soul
Your comfort really is the only comfort that could tame the dark within me
Your happiness would truly give me such joy
And, oh your peace, well for that I would give you a lifetime of gratitude
Dear mind of mine, what say you?
Will you give us another try?

S.K. Mustafa

@s_k_mustafa

Untitled

my adrenaline spiked,
it's now fight or flight
my body can't take any more
perceiving a danger
from some total stranger
as I breathe hard
and look to the floor

day in and day out
I internally shout
and scream to be freed from this hell
relationships strained
my whole being drained
from the toll that it takes to stay well

from whence comes the pain
that drills through my brain?
is it hidden, never to be found?
No, simply that never,
In this life I lead, EVER
am I free from the torment of
S O U N D

it rustles and crunches
through lessons and lunches
and beats me until I am weak
this irrational fear
and my sensitive ear
make existence nothing but bleak

but what can be done?
there is nowhere to run,
no quiet safe place behind glass
so I try to tune in
to a calmness within
and persuade myself
This
Too
Shall
Pass

@effie_neige_words

Darkness Falls

Depression drowns,
Drains devastatingly,
Disparaging dreams,

All too often the colors of my world fade to black. I walk through life seemingly fine, but there is an oppressive weight that tears at my soul. My brain becomes enveloped by fog; I struggle to understand/complete even the simplest of tasks. Mentally & physically I am a shell of who I used to be. I constantly fail to live up to expectations, and that only fuels my self-doubt. Depression is not a choice; one cannot simply "snap out of it." Taking a pill or going to therapy does not make it all better. It is a lifelong battle, and today I am waging war.

@theangelinthedarkness

Diamond in the Rough

Stones
of heart
imperfect, blemished, rise
atop slush, a glorious
Lotus!
hearts broken,
thriving in sunshine
reveal sparkling, rough polished,
Diamonds 💎

~~~~~~~~~~~~~~~~

©@awriterscomeback

I Remembered

I froze that night; I was vulnerable, yet bold,
I Rummaged through a chest; a flashback foretold.
Begging to slam shut psychological abuse,
As my depleted childhood was no longer in use.
An attic search yielded fruitful results,
The outcome of which I couldn't fault.
I stroked the coat's softness; it caressed my cheek,
Then came the thunder strike, like the moon did speak.
The warmth of the coat on that cold night,
Lacked in the years prior; in broad daylight.
Why was I intent on closure's sojourn?
Maybe in hell, I wished the bitch to burn.
If only I'd defied my tormentor then,
She was a well-rounded bitch, some called her Breanne.
My coat's grass stain had smudged her face,
A memory embedded; I could easily trace.
I look at my hands; they're not childlike now,
I won't take crap; I WILL NOT BOW!
I've grown new paths built on a tsunami of fears,
I'm an adult now; I have been for years,
Bullying leaves scars; I still remember those tears.
Bullies today, please hear my plea,
Your children in future may be unlucky.
To escape bullying and it's terrible ways,
During the life term of your kids school days,
Teach them resilience, friendship and hope,
And school days then will be easier to cope.

@poetry_by_effie

Reeling

Reeling
Here I am, swayed
Plummeting through space and time waiting for you to grasp this wretched pendulum
and swing again
Dare I desire the high but dread the low
To and fro
To and fro
End this silly misery
Take me to a place inside your chest for me to know
Let me find the place inside mine so that I may be worthy of love again
I shall not be consumed by nothingness
Shall not surrender my veins to the teeth of you
This life will be the dance I deserve, if partly in darkness.
Dare I?
Dance, I shall.

@aliasjanepoetry

She had a Fault of 3

First was to conceive me
Second was to keep me
And 3rd , the worst of them yet to be
What to birth me

Only these 3 acts should she be punished for
Only these 3 acts gives one the esteemed right of placing the shroud of blame upon her unsupportive shoulders

It was destiny that brought me here and damn that witch has to take me out

For the scars my skin is being abused with scream words I'm no longer willing to listen to

The echo, it's vibration, it has shaken the floor beneath my brittle ankles

I no longer stand tall, I no longer stand able to hold my weight, it's weight, your weight or even hers

I was always the punching bag and I guess it felt good
It numbed my own pain, but now it's creating it
He was always right, always better me, more godly, more moral, perfect for you I guess

I screamed and cut and cried and smiled and starved, I STARVE , just to be an inch closer to you

I was quiet and still, I was loud and proud, I was weak and unable, I was strong and confident, I was godly and I was a sinner, I was a self harmer, I was a worshipper of the body, of the eating disorder, a salve of anxiety and a beautiful queen of depression and yet none of it was enough....

Enough to earn your embrace because you wanted to, to earn your love because you wanted to, to earn your attention because you wanted to
To earn your smile or approval, your acceptance, your light and your love that you gave to everyone else...

They were always just some how better and I was always a retched animal

They could kill and you would love, they would inflict pain yet it was my job to forgive, and if I stood tall on the side of my CUT SCARS I was disrespectful, it was their due right

I would make mistakes, according to their perception and you would strike, once for him, twice for him, and 3 Times for him

Yet he could publicly scream and defame and mock and degrade and ridicule my mind, my demons, my soul, my scars and pain in the presence of such intimate genes and such cold strangers and you would defend him, as if the decision of heaven and hell for you depended on it
But it's true

She had a fault of 3

First was to conceive me
Second was to keep me
And 3rd, the worst of them yet to be
What to birth me

And me? I had a fault of be

To be, me,
My fault lies in the oxygen my lungs selfishly takes in and carbon dioxide it destructively passes on to life so delicate so pure and innocent

Evil I am, for I did not abide

I have a fault of one

The act of not committing suicide
@anorexicmuslimgirl

The Light Inside

Neglected flowers
Still can flourish

And tended flowers
Still can die

Sometimes it's not from things surrounding
But from the light we grow inside

Soak in all you have been gifted
Grateful for the warmth and care
Let it reach your core and renew
In turn, to nourish with all you share

Storms and seasons of solitude
Pass by and test upon our souls
Existing in a loneliness
That fractures once what you thought whole.

But as the vines do seek the water
And as the vines do seek the light
The heart that beats from deep within
Will bloom and flower through this night

~ Heather
@heatherdovey

Wonder

I wonder...

Have you felt them too?
Those deep and heavy currents
which ripple to the surface
of your thoughts,
as the last stray fragments of
pink, purple, and golden twilight sky
disappear over the horizon?

Have you felt it too?

The warm and soft
caress of the morning breeze on your skin?
As amber sunrise encroaches
upon the celestial sphere,
the deepest tides recede;
and with them,
those impressions of the day prior.

I wonder...

A. I. Myles @athenaeumthoughts

Making of Me

After all this time
I finally see
That all of these scars
Were the making of me.

@morethanjustatindergirl

Stalemate

I don't want to life right now
Just want to curl up in the blankets and hide
Feels like I breathed in glass again
Swallowed a damn balloon again
The sand that's still stuck from before is sticking
It's filling
Wounds are slicing back open and the air just can't get in
I hear it all
I see it
I feel it
The words are racing and fighting and clashing in an endless loop
It's her
It's him
I love her
I love him
No, I don't mean this
I do
But not then
Lines are blurred
I'm stirred
I can't turn off this movie in my head
Tick, tick, tick, tick, tick, tick, tick, tick
Can someone please turn off the fucking clock?
I can't breathe
My heart is going to beat itself out of my chest
The demons are unearthed again
They're never going to let me rest
I take ten steps forward
I think I'm finally beginning to heal
I paint on a smile
I allow myself to start to feel
I get close
I make friends
Then I'm suddenly retreating
Because I'm triggered again
I'll never be able to forgive him
I still can't speak his name
But I hate him even more
Every time we play this fucking game
Because he haunts me
No matter how hard I try
I can't get passed him
The monster that just won't die
Is this a movie?
Am I in a horror flick?

How many sequels is this?
And how the hell do I quit?
I swear I'm trying
I'm trying to breathe
I'm trying to live
I'm trying to ME
And I know
I know they don't know
Because I don't tell
No one knows
It's my own private Hell
So when that switch flips
And I just can't breathe
The fucking triggers
The twitching, the screams
They don't know why I cry
They don't know why I freeze
They don't know
What this shit does inside of me
And the glass
Deep inside of my lungs
The pressure
As the darkness succumbs
I don't know who I'm fooling
I'm so far from healed
Hello, PTSD
I can't keep you sealed
Might as well greet you
Since you're clearly here to stay
I'd shake your hand
But everything already shaking anyway
I can't escape you
The noose clenched on my throat
The knife on my flesh
You laugh and you gloat
As I crumble
I shrivel and shrink
No air can get in
But it's easy to drink
I just keep pouring
Trying to drown you out
Wishing for darkness
Silence the shouts
I'm always haunted
Can't escape his face
I'd scratch off my eyelids
If I thought it would change

Burn down this nightmare
That once was a home
He never lived here
But yet, he still roams
Just like my shadow
Always following me
I can't escape this
I'll never be free
Splay myself unto the altar
Fucking exorcise me!
I've had my fill
I've suffered enough
So many years
Without human touch
He ruined me well
His damage a true work of art
I'm so tired now
Someone please take my heart
I do not want it
Not anymore
Not with him in it
It's too much to ask for
I breathe in sawdust
Exhale razors again
Another night shaking whispers
I just can't win.

@inktswords

Untitled

one day you will open your eyes
you'll no longer fear waking up
to a sunny morning
you'll smile
followed behind
will be the love of your life
there will be sunshine on your face
and a warm feeling in your heart
you are home
you will realize
you had to go through the bad
to be right where you are
you fought storms
to get to paradise
so the day you open your eyes
don't question it
just love
so many can't wait to greet you

@abbey_writes -Abbey Michelle

No Such Thing as Crazy

warped voices above
unbendable sheets

files and folders
determine my fate

hurrying footsteps
up and down
up and down

strangers with lanyards
fake friendship
whisper conspiracies

do they think I'm stupid?

torchlight eyes
through the night
on off on off

lunchtime, I watch while
my body stays in bed

Pink Dress delivers
poisoned food

the devil on the altar
at my feet, smiles

immovable potato mash
no knife to cut the flapping fish
stiff jelly in sea-melt ice cream

in the courtyard
lop-sided netball hoop
slumps exhausted

in my head
in my head
ready to run
watch for the open door

goodbye walls
hello freedom

cigarette smoke loops 'escape'
drifting on a breeze,
to anywhere but here.

@sarabruxner

A Little Reminder

When you've burnt me down
so my flesh is grey,
When you've drained me of blood
so my strength would stray,
When you've crushed my weary bones
day after day,
There's something you'll witness
that terrifies prey,
There's something ancient
that fights like thunder in the fray,
There's something inside
that lights my way,
There's lightning in my eyes,
the kind that never dies.

@captain_subtle

Drowning

I am drowning again in my own battles
with old grief and new sorrows.
the moon gifted me on the night I was born.
The sun chose to ignore my plea for salvation,
the wind was never ever present,
she was too busy drifting between planets
where life didn't even exist.
I've forgotten what they've taught me
in the swimming classes, people usually go to,
you know where you are told to sit on a chair
and take in deep breaths,
with the palms faced upwards on your laps
as if you are holding the air you just exhaled
like you would hold a newborn child.
I came here to learn how to push through
the strong currents of a particular sea,
a sea of depression and misery.
Each time I plunge in, my limbs won't move,
I'm frozen in one spot, too afraid to even try.
I just wait for someone to notice,
the top of my head, popping in and out
of the cold waters, hoping they'd dive in
and pull me out to safety.
I hear my instructors yelling my name
each time I refuse to sway my hands
in circular motions, but would they understand?
Would they be willing to hear the sounds,
echoing in the inside of my head?
So loud it can make your ears bleed
with just one scream.
Drowning,

I am still drowning can't you see?
I'll keep at it till the bottom touches my feet
What am I planning to do you ask?
I am starting all over again,
from underneath.

@mad_story_teller

Prism of Hope

Peering dimly through window panes
darkened with dusty despair,
and cracked from dreams' destitution,
you mourn the forlorn prophecy
of a forsaken future.
You mourn the loss of zeal.
You mourn the loss of passion.
You mourn the loss of love.

But I'll share mine.

And I'll share my hands
to help you build again.
And I'll share my voice
to help you sing again.
And I'll share my faith
to help you believe again.

The heart of a caring friend
beating in time with yours.
Fingertips touching,
igniting a spark,
waning willpower awakens to a new dawn.
The dirty window
becomes brilliant stained glass,
washed with colors radiating
from a prism of hope
and sun-kissed saturation.

Shadows evaporate;
the path forward is revealed,
paved with promise,
heralded by birdsong.

Hey...

Smile...

It can happen,
and it will.

@tagramere

The Hottest Day

Sun-baked,
Caked in sweat.
Dirt beneath my fingernails.
The cat sleeps under the rhubarb patch as the
Skin on my shoulders sears
And begins to peel.
Feel everything.
Feel it all.
The call of the wild earth and fire.
It is alive and so am I.
I never thought I'd get here.
That's not hyperbolic poetic license,
I just
Never saw the life line on my palm
Stretch as far as this island of calm.
I could never feel the pull of a future,
Could never see a shore worth
Fighting against the tide for,
And yet -
Here we are,
Laying on our backs in the meadow-sweet grass.
Hold on, dear heart.
Hold on.
I promise,
The living will start.

@alicewroteit

A Poem on Mental Health

You are not the only bird with broken wings
You are not the only body bound with tenebrous strings,
You are not the only one that got shattered by destiny.
You are not the only one to live in Stygian gloom, with despondency and fear!
I know you don't belong here.
Nothing seems fair!
Nothing seems clear!
You question your own identity,
Your mind seems to be your worst enemy!
You are not alone here!
I too have travelled these dark satanic places, where I shouldn't have been.
This was the worst I had seen.
Hold my hand now that you have heard me sing!
Let's together heal our debilitated spirits!
There is an effulgent life on the other side of this vast sea of desolation.
Come! Embrace that effulgence ,
This is your moment; This is your redemption.
The whole universe is here to espouse your resolution.
Lets embark on this journey to heal our enervated souls,
Lets cross this sea together and again make ourselves complete and whole.

@golden_skript

Who I Am

Everything I behold
that which continues to grow
to create my reality
to allow my old self to overthrow,
these feelings
that have held me back
that have prevented me from dealing
with what has risen to the surface
and impended my dreaming.
So many years of ignoring,
these thoughts buried deep
but oh this sense of liberation
to let go and allow that side to sleep.
To feel my roots go deeper
to draw up more power each day,
the freedom in realizing
this new empowered me is here to stay.
Even in my exhaustion
I can tap into my source
and connect with this energy
and allow myself to reinforce
that which is my right
to be proud of whom I am
to hold my head up high
and say to all I don't give a damn,
for your opinions and disapproval
for how you think I should behave,
I have embraced myself
and I will not be enslaved.
@trucklifefamily

Trauma is my Muse

Trauma is the tightrope;
We tiptoe across
From the meagre to mountain
We have found in the molehill,

Trauma has no full stop;

It keeps on our heels,
Lurks in the corner
And curve of
wall shadows,

Breathes down our necks
Smelling of malt
and nail varnish remover,
Mouthwash and remorse
Trauma is a liar,
That whispers time heals,
Between drumbeat tick tocks
Of not-healing time-clocks

Trauma is the sound of keys,
A land line phone ring
With bad news,
The sound of ragged breaths
Or muffled screams,
The taste of a bitten tongue;
A metallic sip of iron drip,
A panic-bubble in the throat

Trauma is the trigger
Pulled by devastating
Details of the mundane,
Missed by most,
For their own pain
Is jolted back to life
By a different strain
Of mauve or toffee or rain
But despite this,
Trauma is our muse;
A moonbeam in our darkness,
A melting frost
In our low and lost,
A whisper of a simile,
Like a rosebud through broken glass;

Trauma is the sensory reminder
We are not the victim
But the survivor,
Here to create our art,
And soothe the screams
In someone else's triggered heart.

@unseen_unheard_poet

Untitled

a storm
It lurked
Then struck
And took my breath away
But after awhile
I got back up
They hit you
The storms
But you forget that
There may be another one
Just beyond the bend
That will leave you struggling
For something to
Believe in
Something to hang on to
But this time
I learned
To breathe beyond the collar bone
And into the abdomen where anxiety
Is banished and peace begins

@bleeshor

Change the Game

This giant wheel won't stop!
It might, but only momentarily
Just giving me enough time
To get my bearings
For the next ride
Which is just round the corner.
I can feel the gears shift
As I'm slowly raised up high.
Reluctantly, forcibly moving,
Against gravity, against my wishes.
I know that moments from now,
Its all going downhill!
When I'm at the very top,
The wheel pauses...
Just for a minute,
While another hapless soul hops on.
All I want then in that moment is,
To fling myself from the top
I'm desperate to get off this ride,
I freeze when I remember
The magnitude of what's at stake!
I have to hold on can't let go,
Right now, all I can do
Is brace myself for the fall.
I've done it so many times now,
That I know the exact point,
At which my gut will be wrenched,
My insides twisted and contorted,
The bile in my belly,
Will rush up to my throat.
I'm filled with a feeling
Of utter and sheer helplessness,
My head spins wildly
My eyes are shut tight,
While my ears pick laughter,
From the merry people in the fair.
I've never felt more distant,
From the world around me
When I hear the sounds of glee
I wonder how and why am I here?
Why the world goes about
In a normal sort of way,
While I spin round and round each day?
I never bought a ticket
I never signed up for the ride

The only way this wheel will stop
Is when I let my insecurities drop
Look around the fair, people everywhere
Find a soul that seems to care
Share your fears, give anxiety a name
Empower yourself to change the game

☆Asmita Patwardhan

@foundavoice

An Invitation

If you have a moment to spare
Take my hand
We'll climb onto a sliver of hope
Glide across the green still
Lose our selves in twisted mangroves
Selves peeled one petal at a time
Released gently to the sun
Till all that's left
Is the sound of this heart on this river.

@lipstickandmiracles

Simplicity, oddly enough

Often-days she functions properly, whole days (or for most of the days) Simplicity seems everything. Life itself an easy task. Not even as a word within her mind does confusion exist: Unheard of, unknown, right is right and left is – up and down is – back and sideways – halt - suddenly, in the middle of whatever there is no ground, middle or otherwise nothing to hold onto, to hold the mind up, to hold the brain: As if it suddenly shed its housing, nothing there to encase thoughts, keep them in line, their line-up existing no longer strictly as a function for clarity in simplicity. Simplicity itself abruptly loses all meaning. No knowledge of the word, unheard of. Confusion reigns without being named the culprit, since confusion confuses itself and her brain, which cannot differentiate any longer between itself and the ins or outs of what it is to be, to be a brain, a functioning mind a body, a person, a whole. She herself doesn't comprehend herself existing. She's a nil in a void in a nothing of tumble-weed threads of thought leading nowhere other than in on themselves (Who can ever tell what exists, anyway) Life itself incomprehensible of course: The simplicity of complexity.

@roberthludwig

Stop/Start

I stopped worrying
Cause it gave me heartaches
I stopped crying
Cause it gave me headaches
I started praying
Cause it gave me a break!
Sometimes we gotta stop
before we start!

@joannethepoetess

It's All in my Head

I was told: it's all in my head….

Sometimes I lie on my bed,
Remembering the lies I was fed
'Til my desires were dead
Yet they said: it's all in my head

My heart is torn to shreds
all I hear is whispers of dread
Sometimes I wish I had fled
Yet they say: it's all in my head

I am always to blame
my excuses, they call lame
treating my realities like it's a game
yet they say: it's all in my head

they shackled me with expectations
binding me with mystical speculations
I am a prisoner of formulated allegations
yet they say: it's all in my head

If it's all in my head
why isn't there cure in all you have said?
for my ears are an entry way to my head
why are you not listening to all I have said?

yes, it's all in my head
so everyday I get up from my bed
letting my heart be the led
not your voices in my head

you were told: it's all in your head

@creozoe_ink

Grave-ful

How do you thank one,
Who keeps you alive;
Pumps your heart like,
Love at first sight;
Shields you from stinging,
November rain;
Calms your subconscious,
From screaming so strange?

You give them your ghost-
A rose on their grave.

-Lady Leigh
@ladyleighpoetry

I Want

The sun kisses the horizon good morning //and a new day begins. //A day filled with promise //newly born to this world //like a babe delivered from the womb. //

I sit and watch the sun greet the day; //a fiery ball sitting on the rim //of a young morning. // I want to feel reborn. //I want to be okay.

@keboriginals

Smile Once More

It hurts that you didn't
Want to be with me today

When I reached out for your
Touch, you turned away

Written over your face were
Only thoughts of dismay

I hope you can smile
At me again someday

N.C. Mercer
@imagineexplorecreate

The World Needs Your Precious Petals

Whenever you feel sad and blue. Remember He's there every step of the way.
The strains of life's trials and tribulations makes you feel anxious, and down.

Remember He's always beside you. Try to think of the positive things that you are blessed with in life.
This shall pass, the mood shall also pass, it will rise with a ray of hope with The Almighty's help.

Whenever you feel sad or alone, or anxious. Remember that He shall heal your hearts and comfort you.

Things will get better in time, always remind yourself 'I am not alone', the one who's knows me best; will always protect me and keep me safe and well.

The sun shall too will come shining through.

Be strong and hold on tight to the rope of God and never let it go.

Everything in life has an appointed time and place. Keep trust in God and faith.

@sairathepoet

Untitled

Slowly he slips back into the corner
Dark spaces are touching every border
The room spins and he is in delight
This is his definition of good night
The house falls back to earth
Rearranged, the time has slipped
Hearts beat no one is skipped
Tales fascinate, to the crowds delight
No one notices there's no sunlight
The darkness, isn't so scary after all
But don't be so brazen in your relaxed state
There's no telling what's beyond the gates
Heaven or hell, to each his own views
Be careful, what you think out loud isn't always what you'll choose
The webs we weave and the torment we inflict, resides in our mind's eye eating at the conscience and whispers softly from our lips
Dreams never escape, stuck locked inside
Once again the drugs blind the mind's eye.
Blanketing the hurt like a loving mothers hugs
Truths buried in dirt, they're swept beneath the rug
The lies leak from your brain, released from your mouth leaving permanent stains on your tainted reputation
The guilt eats at you, your mind an infestation
You look over your shoulders, resisting this daily temptation
The thoughts get stronger with each passing day
The stress won't relent, making you pay
The sins of a life you don't recall choosing
The answer is so simple, yet so beautifully confusing
Because you feel like dying, while everything around you is blooming
One day at a time tomorrow will be better, it's the last string you have to hold onto and you hold for dear life.
But tomorrow never arrives, so for today you'll survive.

J. Steele
@joesteele401

Bitter Words

I said I loved you to death.
You said I was nothing
without you.

You tried to make sure
I kept those words,
but you ate yours first
when I survived
to love me.

That is everything.

A. Shea

@a.shea_writer

Hearth of Hope

Sunkissed are the skies outside
While dark clouds are pouring on me,
Thoughts crashing like high tides on rocks
But stop, my heart isn't that strong.
Murky water of memories flowing from
the crack of my hearts,
Like an ebony waterfall contaminated.
Heart loses and fall,
Curled up under the stars, sprinkled in disarray,
Like the scatter lines of fate,
in my lily white palm.
Heart withering, weeping
Like a Sunflower ashen, in sunlight
Heart on her knees, begging
For hope to ignite and praying to get healed.
Aching to shivers
Like the remnants of waning moon
In numbed sorrow of time.
As hope caresses the sobbing heart,
Drinking her tears, hope kisses her forehead
And begins to stitch her scars with string of love eternal
Cuddling cradling? her in warmth,
It says,
Hang in there,
Fate is in the prayers of broken hearts.

-Ayshah K. Ayris
@whispersofbrokenheart

Freedom

Freedom is something we take for granted, but imagine bring denied freedom by the one person who should want it most; Yourself.

It started to take over my life and have a huge impact on my mental and physical health.

Everything from sleeping, walking and reading influenced by fear.
If everything wasn't done exactly right, terrible things would happen to everyone I hold dear.

Paralysed by what if questions and wanting everything to be in our control.
Our mind taking us prisoner and refusing to give us parole.
You may question your sanity and whether you'll get your life back.
Letting negative thoughts take over and focusing on what our lives may lack.

I'm here to tell you though, that your thoughts are not as powerful as you think.
You are the captain of the ship and can change direction before it sinks.
I know sometimes you feel like no one knows what you're going through, but I can assure you that you're not alone.
We spent years without OCD and can get back to that, your path is changeable and is not set in stone.

@a.o.ewen

Biographies

In this section of the book we have the biographies of the poets in the book who wished to share their bios.

Each bio explains a little about the poet with a note on the page number of their poem, for ease of finding.

Saira Anwar

Saira Anwar resides in Manchester, England. She writes and speaks from the heart sharing her life lessons and experiences with creativity. To heal broken hearts with peace, love and light. You can find her work on instagram at @sairathepoet

Anorexic Muslim Girl

Her name ... well she doesn't really know what it is, but what she can tell you is that it doesn't define her. That she is made up of battle scars... come and join her as she raises them to the sky for the angels to gaze upon. You can find her work on instagram at @anorexicmuslingirl

Shravani P.T.

She is the girl who quit law to write for a living. She uses words to rationalize her eccentricity. And the fire that won't stay content in her belly. She Lives in Delhi, the heart of India. You can find her work on instagram at @julyblossom23

Sharon Andrews

Sharon is a lover of reading and writing. She lives in West Sussex with her husband and has grown up children. She has a poetry collection called "Inksomnia" available on Amazon. You can find her work on instagram at @shandrewspoetry

Jo Kingston

Jo Kingston lives in Piha, New Zealand (a Wild West Coast surf beach). She is a mom of three and many animals. In between teaching full time she writes poetry and plays music; both of which are her therapy. You can find her work on instagram at @amusemeamuseisme

Sharron Green

Sharron Green from Guildford, England describes herself as a menopausal empty nester. As @rhymes_n_roses she enjoys sharing her poetry, which combines nostalgia and attempts to make sense of modern life. Although many of her subjects are serious, she tries to inject humour and positivity - and sometimes succeeds. You can find her work on instagram at @rhymes_n_roses

Kelly Gourdreau

Edmonton, Alberta based poetess, Kelly Goudreau, began her writing journey in high school and hasn't put her pen down since. Each poem she writes may vary in style, but always comes straight from her soul. You can find her on Instagram @poeticpiper

Void_vis_vires

Lonely Artificial intelligence turned poet
Neurodiverse mental health advocate.
Aloof but loving.
Find more @void_vis_vires on instagram

Kayt Rozdzek

Kayt Rozdzek is a poet, nerd, cat servant and much more. Her writing is dark with a twist of whimsy and realism due to her constant battle with mental illness. You can find her work on instagram @kayt_of_wands

Asmita Patwardhan

Asmita Patwardhan is from India and has been writing poetry and sharing it on her Instagram account " foundavoice" for the past two years. To throw light her process and her work she can only quote herself "The best part about poetry is that it says it all except saying exactly what it needs to say. It's a catharsis that holds back as much as it lets loose. You can find more of her work on instagram @foundavoice

O.O Akinyele

O.O Akinyele is a 22-year-old poet who lives in Nigeria. Whenever he's not writing or reading, he's planning on going on yet another adventure. He shares his poems on his Instagram page with the handle @yelewrites

Joanne F Blake

Joanne F Blake is a poetic writer and professional caregiver. She is currently working on publishing her first children's book on bullying. She lives in her hometown Augusta, Ga with her husband and family.
Her writings are on instagram as @joannethepoetess

Sunil Sathyendra

Sunil Sathyendra aka Pungidasa is an engineer by profession and writer by passion, who firmly believes that words and emotions are his window to connect with people in the world. Hailing from India's busy city of Bengaluru, he has published four books until now in the poetry and short-stories genre. You can find more of his work on instagram @sunilsathyendra

Stephanie Warrillow

Stephanie Warrillow liveS in Scotland. She suffers with depression and anxiety. You can find more of her work on instagram @poemsbystephanie1

Mary E

Mary E (they/them) is a queer, non-binary poet who believes that pockets of magic exist everywhere. They take multiple brain medications and can't imagine life without them. Find them @maryewrites on instagram, twitter, or tumblr where they're probably talking about poetry, coffee, or their family.

Bonnie Shor

Bonnie writes to fill the hole in her heart created by the suicide of her younger son. She has come alive again according to her sister. His memory is a blessing. You can find more of her work on instagram @bleeshor

K.M. Lennan

K.M. Lennan, known to her friends as Katie (or Kt) is an American writer and poet. Katie views writing on the same level as breathing, it's a necessary and essential part of her life. She began writing creatively at a very early age as a means of coping and extracting the thoughts in her head she couldn't otherwise speak. Words have saved her countless times. Katie's words can be found on Instagram under the handle @inktswords

Anu

Anu is an aspiring writer who loves to create art across mediums. She is a Scientist by profession, sassy by nature and a Scorpio by heart. She has dubbed herself as FairySassMother and is always happy to be your personal cheerleader anytime you are in need of one. You can find her at @allyouneedisalilbitofsugar.

Scott Mckenzie

Scott Mckenzie, the captain of nonsense. He sails through the universe of poetry, using words to reflect inwards, outwards, and roundabouts. A very big thank you goes to the creator of this collection of poems for putting together such a wonderful project. You can find more of his work on instagram @captain_subtle

Kait Quinn

Kait Quinn is a law admin by day and a prolific poet by night. She studied creative writing at St. Edward's University in Austin, TX and her poetry has been published in Sorin Oak Review and New Literati. She is also the author of the poetry collection A Time for Winter. Kait currently lives in Minneapolis with her partner and their regal cat Spart. You can find her work on instagram @kaitquinnpoetry

Christina Triplett-Wagenknecht

Christina Triplett-Wagenknecht is an amateur poet originally from Florida. Since 2008, she has been writing from Germany, where she lives with her husband. She has been featured on several poetry sites, and you can find her running, "Prompt-A-Palooza" on Instagram, under @ladyleighpoetry. She has several mental illnesses, induced by past traumas, so much of her poetry expresses struggles surrounding this theme, including self-neglect."

Josepha

Josepha goes simply by JoJo. Writing for her has always been one of the few ways she could express herself. Her muse usually comes from her life experiences and everyday activities such as music, art, books, photography. But lately her work has really been inspired by B.T.S (Bangtan Sonyeondan) — She is a huge fan of their work. You can find more of her work on instagram @_kimenyembo_

Swell Versed

Swell Versed is a lifelong poet aspiring to inspire with her unique rhythmic rhymes, which are artistic expressions of her professional "creative problem-solver" voice. You can more of her work on instagram @swellversed

Janani

Janani is a self-taught artist, poet, mother and an entrepreneur from Bangalore, India. Words and colours have formed the crux of her world since childhood. She writes in various poetic forms on a wide range of topics, often emanating her strong opinions, emotions on societal issues and her unique perspective on life. You can find more of her work on instagram @pennyformythoughts_

Arotuy

Shae Hendrix is an aspiring writer living in Germany and trying to survive her own thinking process.

She strives on words and sharing her work online. She's also travelled quite a few places and yet never managed to acquire more than two languages, which is a shame, but she still managed to fall in love with getting lost in a good book on sleep deprived nights.
You can find more of her work on instagram @arotuy

Widaad Pangarker

She can be found near cats, books, water and popcorn. She's been writing since she could hold a crayon, and writes because she breathes. She's had a play staged in a National Theatre in South Africa and has had prose and poetry published in literary journals locally and abroad. You can find more of her work on instagram @widwords

Effie_neige_words

effie_neige_words aka Jen is a Mum, Voice Teacher and poet from Essex. Writing poetry and free verse has been invaluable in her own mental health journey, and this subject matter is often present in her work. She performs at poetry events in Essex and London. You can find more of her work on Instagram @effie_neige_words

Neha Taneja

Three things Neha Taneja is passionate about are Geography, Teaching and Poetry. She is currently a facilitator at Salwan Public School, New Delhi. Neha completed her BA and MA in Geography from Visva Bharati University Santiniketan followed by an M.Phil from Delhi School of Economics. Her passion for reading led her to pen poems, her debut book Under the Crimson Sky was published in 2018. Other books she has co-authored include Wildflower Rising, Train River Poetry, Taste her mind. To read more of her work follow her on Instagram @neha.m.taneja.

Taylor Tippins

Taylor Tippins is a gemini, actress, poet, candle maker, moon worshipper, dog/cat mom, and forest mother to many squirrels, birds, & chipmunks. My favorite author is Edgar Allan Poe. You can find more of her work on Instagram @geminiandthewolf

Joe Steele

Joe Steele is a poet from Rhode Island, USA. His upbringing and his hometown are a big part of his writing. He writes with passion and emotion and intensity. He prides himself on being honest, thoughtful and most of all fearless. You can find more of his work on Instagram @joesteele401

Mayank Barman

Mayank Barman is a poet from India. His poems describe the things and phases people go through in their lives, which change their perception altogether and maybe inspire them along the way.

You can find him on his Instagram page :- @Viralvirus_official.

John

John lives in Liverpool UK with his rock and soul mate fiancé Lisa, along with their two beautiful young children.

John has suffered with his mental health from a young age. Poetry helps him to vent and so often decipher a lot of the thoughts and feelings that until picking up a pen were just white noise.

When someone can relate to his words he says that he appreciates their magic even more. You can find more of his work on Instagram @scarlarjpoetic

Dolly Sangwaiya

Dolly Sangwaiya hails from India, she specializes in English literature major, her poems speak her heart as she considers poetry her escape, she is currently working on her debut poetry book. You can find more of her work on Instagram @poetrybydolly

Sweedle D'souza

Sweedle D'souza is an HR assistant by profession and a writer by heart.

When she is not writing, she loves to read, indulge in community service, journaling and decluttering with a minimalistic approach.

She has published her debut book "A butterfly called hope " in 2018. You can find her book on Amazon. You can find more of her work on Instagram @mad_story_teller.

Sana Adhikari Chhetri

Sana Adhikari Chhetri aka Sanapoet is from Nepal, she is a physical therapist and a writer. She mostly puts her words to create vague expressions in poems and storytelling. You can find more of her work at Instagram @sana_poet

Zee

Zee is a 21 year old desert native living in the Pacific Northwest. They are a college student majoring in Psychology. Through their art and writing, they strive to connect with the most visceral parts of the human condition. When Zee isn't writing, you might find them tending to their plant babies, crocheting, or looking for the places where the light pours in. You can find more of their work on Instagram @writingpoemsinthedark

Sophia

Sophia is a homemaker from Pakistan. She is in love with words. Being overly sensitive, she feels everything going on in her surroundings, in nature and in this world. She just wants to spread awareness and raise issues that are being neglected through her poetry. She believes in lifting up people through her words. You can find more of her work on Instagram @confessions_of_sophia

Julie Onoh

Julie Onoh is a Nigerian author who firmly believes that writers can make a positive difference in the world through words. When she's not weaving tales of lost kingdoms in her head, you can find her writing poetry on her instagram page @julieonohwrites

Jahanvi D

An anxious over-thinker like Jahanvi knows how twisted one's mind can get. So to whoever reads this, they wish you inner peace and calm.

Instagram handle: @poetryinparis

Sarahlyn D. Revillo

Sarahlyn D. Revillo, is a working professional and a collector of words from the Philippines. Her writings are mostly inspired by the experiences in her journey towards learning self-love, in the hopes that others may learn from this too. When asked why she began publishing her works in an anthology account, she answered, "I figured that there's no better way to exercise this passion I have for writing than invoke even the slightest bit of emotion and awareness. I used to treat writing as a form of escape but I don't want to just escape, anymore, I want to get involved." You can find more of her work on Instagram @ollivernylpoetry_

Jane

Poetry inspired by love, lust and PTSD.
Currently working on a series of children's books based on my last 14 years working with clients with Autism. You can find more of her work on Instagram @aliasjanepoetry

Gina Rivera-Garza

Gina Rivera-Garza has been writing since she was 12 years old. The reason why she writes is because over the years she has gone through many things that cause depression, anxiety, ptsd, as well as suicide. My writings tend to help her explore her thoughts and emotions she felt or is feeling at a certain time in her life. She hopes her writings can help people see that they are not alone when struggling with their mental health. You can find more of her work on Instagram@_darkness.within.

Asta Lander

Asta Lander is an Australian artist and writer who lives with her husband and animal companions on a 3 acre property in picturesque Margaret River. You can find more of her work on Instagram @asta_lander_art

Darrel Gibbs

Darrel is from Australia and he has been diagnosed with CPTSD, chronic anxiety, depression and ADHD. Writing helps him to help others, and helping others helps him. You can find more of his work on Instagram @the_illiterate_poet70

Elise Emersyn

Elise Emersyn is a high school teacher and poet from Northeast Pennsylvania in the United States. Her debut book of poetry, Drowning Back to Life, was published in 2018 by Blind Faith Books and is available on Amazon. She is also a curator for Pack Poetry, and has been featured on numerous Instagram poetry platforms as well as a poem on a bus panel in Northeast PA that was accepted through an initiative called Poetry in Transit. You can find more of her work on Instagram @eliseemersynpoetry

Julesieelle

Julesieelle is a poet from North London.
Her interests are varied, she makes jewellery, loves reading and baking and learning something new every day. You can find more of her work on instagram @julesieelle

Invisibleme

A shy poet, hence the Instagram handle, working in London. She secretly writes about life experiences, the world around her & matters close to the heart. You can find more of her work on Instagram @invisibleme

Aiyesha

Aiyesha is 18 years old and she write poetry. She is passionate about each of these verses and her only hope is they provide solace and comfort to everyone suffering with mental health. You can find more of her work on Instagram @aiyesha_

Heather Dahlquist (Holzrichter)

The reason Heather started writing was to give voice to who she was hidden inside. To share the strength she found there, and the hope it kindled in the future. To teach her children and encourage others that the struggles we endure are not all there is to life. But to find happiness in the little things and always look for the spark within, to light the path ahead. You can find more of her work on Instagram @heatherdovey

Timi Jolaoso

Timi is a Nigeria born Canadian poet. An engineer, graphic designer, and brand owner. He loves God, creating life through graphics, writing and photography. You can find more of his work on Instagram @creozoe_ink

Robert Ludwig Hess

Having lived in Hessen, Germany, working in the county's capital, Wiesbaden, at the City's State Theatre since the Eighties, Robert Ludwig Hess writes poetry in English and German.

He finds inspiration in nature and the arts, daily life and human nature.
He aspires to keep fresh and versatile in form and content, ranging from free verse, haiku and tanka to classics like sonnets, encompassing comedy and tragedy. He considers himself a citizen of the world, although his heart found it's true home in Greece, on Crete.

S.R.Chappell

S.R.Chappell lives in Powder Springs, Georgia. Her book "Inked Heart Poetry" can be purchased at Amazon and Kindle. You can follow her on Facebook and Instagram under the name Inked Heart Poetry. She is currently working on her second book "Light Inbetween Darkness", to be released soon.

Patricia Ndombe

Patricia Ndombe is currently an undergraduate poet at North Carolina State University in Raleigh, NC pursuing a major in English and Creative Writing. She enjoys writing poetry as a creative outlet that enables her to reflect the world around her, escape the troubles of life, or look at it through another lens.

Patricia has been blessed with the opportunity to publish over ten poems so far this year. She thanks you for the opportunity to share her work.

Instagram: @poetic.patricia
Twitter: @poeticpatricia
Website: https://sites.google.com/view/poeticpatricia

Emily Salt

Emily Salt is a passionate and quirky poet from Whitby, Ontario, Canada. Her avant-guard approach to writing will inspire reflective thinking, eye-brow raised perspectives, or a good belly laugh. You can find more of her work on Instagram @emilysaltpoetry

Adrian Joseph Concepcion

Adrian is from the Philippines. Music and personal experiences help shape his words into poetry. He gives life to his feelings through writing. You can find more of his work on Instagram @blcklns_aj18

Curtis Edwards

My writing is a very important coping mechanism to me. It allows my mind to pick out some meaning from the noise and gives me agency and power over my mental health. You can find more of his work on Instagram @kurtedwardspoetry

Ghihaad

Ghihaad, means perseverance. Ghihaad lives in South Africa. Her writing is simple, but always authentic to what she believes and feels. She love the picture created by piecing words together, and hopes to write something truly magical someday. You can find more of her work on Instagram @mynamemeans_perseverance

Maria

Maria is a divorced mother of three grown kids and one grandson with another grandchild coming in 2020. She has worked at a state university as a cleaner for the past 17 years. Her hobbies include photography and reading books and writing poetry. You can find more of her work on Instagram @mariawyn316

Stacy Coventry

Stacy Coventry lives in Florida, USA, and writes poetry that covers such themes as depression, heartache, romance, and family. Astronomy, physics, and alchemy make guest appearances, as well. You can find more of he work on Instagram @stacy_coventry_is_here

Erin and Emma

Erin is from Sussex and she is a 24 year old bibliophile, advocate for mental health and Hufflepuff who loves to write poetry, influenced by different moments in her life. Currently studying Criminology at the University of Wolverhampton and living her best life. You can find more of her work on Instagram @baldilockswrites

Emma is 22 and from the Brighton area, currently living in the West Midlands. She love to read, it's her safe haven and have recently started writing, thanks to her partner who inspired her and told her she could. Mental health is a core influence in her life so this was very important to her. You can find more of her work on Instagram @writingsofhairlocks

Amber Jasinski

Amber Jasinski is an RN, wife, and mom of 3, grandma of 2 from Atlanta, Ga. She enjoys writing as an avenue to explore her own journey with mental illness and to promote mental health advocacy. She writes under the name ajblueorion on social media where you'll find her "lost somewhere between the words and melancholy madness.

S.K

S.K is from London, England. She loves to use her writing space to share her emotions and life experiences. One of the things she is most passionate writing about is her experience with anxiety and depression- having readers tell her that they resonate with her words is a wonderful feeling. You can find more of her work on Instagram @s_k_mustafa

Stephen Scanlon

Stephen has been writing for many years now. He never sticks to one genre, as he writes whatever comes to mind on the day.
He also like to write songs on guitar. He lives in south London and his happiest times are spent with family, trying to enjoy life as much as possible. You can find more of his work on Instagram @poetry_viking

Ayshah K. Ayris

Ayshah K. Ayris is a young writer, from Dubai UAE. She's famous on Instagram for her poetry pieces, she loves experimenting with different styles of poem and encourages her readers to see things through her lens. You can find more of her work on Instagram @whispersofbrokenheart

Sonia

Sonia lives in LA and is a business owner. Writing has been a passion since childhood but she only realized how important it is for her to be able to unleash the emotions through this art form. She really feels empowered to use words to express concern for causes that are dear to her. You can find more of her work on Instagram @golden_skript

Grace Stevenson

Grace is a published poet from Quebec, Canada. Her work focuses on love, nature, self discovery and personal growth. You can find more of her work on Instagram@susurruspoetry

Jen Elvy

Jen has always loved writing and in early 2016 she finally found her place in the world of writing; She started writing poetry. To begin with, it was about motherhood but then she began to write about a wider range of topics. Now she writes about life and also she writes fantasy poetry. You can find more of her work @jen.elvy_poems

Amy C. Wheeler

A writer, photographer and intuitive art maker living in Maine, USA. She is driven to map the world as she sees it and is eager to share this view with others one piece of art at a time. You can find more of her work on Instagram @wheelacw32

Josie

Josie is from Las Vegas, Nevada. She just graduated high school and has been writing her whole life. Her poetry has always been about things she faces day to day in her life, like struggling with mental illness. Poetry is her way of coping with these struggles. You can find more of her work on Instagram @l_ove_letters

Aalia Liaquat

Aalia Liaquat known as harvestingmind is from India. She was writing on and off until she joined Instagram in 2019. She mostly enjoys writing love and nature related poems. You can find more of her work on Instagram @harvestingmind

Lindokuhle Mngadi

A South African poet who is fascinated by words and how they go together. He believes that everyone has the ability to write. As long as it is from the heart. You can find more of his work on Instagram @lindodapoet

Robert

Robert started writing in the middle of 2017, partly out of boredom but also having epilepsy, writing helps him deal with the condition while creating an awareness around it. You can find more of his work on Instagram @epilepsy_in_motion

Cheree Alexander-Velez

Cheree Alexander-Velez, pen name Jereni-Sol. Cheree is a published poet and spoken word artist from the Bronx. She has performed at several venues throughout the Bronx and Manhattan, such as the Nuyorican Poet's Café, The Schomburg Library and the Bronx Museum of Arts. Her work can be found in several anthologies including "Bronx Writers Anthology", "Broken Hearts – Healing Words" & "Poetry Pills: A prescription for goodness" You can also find her work on Instagram, Facebook & Twitter: jerenisolpoetry

Angie Waters

Angie Waters is a writer/artist who uses the alias A. Shea. Her work often reflects her own healing process as a trauma survivor as well as her fight to maintain her mental health and live well with chronic illness. You can find her on Facebook at www.facebook.com/a.sheawriter and Instagram @a.sheawriter.

Karen

Karen is a published poet from Texas, USA where she lives with her husband, three dogs, two cats, three horses and five donkeys. Karen has been writing since her teens and has been published in Train River Poetry Winter 2019 Anthology, Poet Speak Magazine Issue 27, "Instagram Poets You'll Want to Follow", and SpillWords Press. She will be self-publishing her first book of poems in 2020 You can find more of her work on Instagram @keboriginals

Devi Chong

Devi is from Guyana. She is honoured for her piece on depression to be featured since it is a topic that is very close to her. It is her hope that it can be a positive influence on anyone suffering from depression and to know that they are not alone in this fight. It is important to always remind ourselves and others that we are all important and loved for in one way or another.

You can find more of her work on Instagram @the_sparrowstories

Carol Longfellow

Carol lives in Scotland with her husband and has 3 grown up children. She loves writing poetry and has been posting for months on IG. She is passionate about raising awareness about mental health issues and supporting people. She writes under Carol's name to protect her identity and give her freedom to write how she feels. You can find more of her work on Instagram @carol_longfellow

Palak (PS)

Palak lives in Denmark and has been writing for 10 years. She loves fantasy and romance and combining it with science and art. An entrepreneur and biotechnologist by profession, she finds solace in the pages of any good book after a day's hard work.

You can find more of her work on Instagram @wordeliciouspoetry

Mari

Mari Antoinette is a poetess with a great love for the writing style, she lives in the Netherlands but feels more at home in the English language. You can find more of her work on Instagram @poetessofhearts

Linda Lokhee

Linda Lokhee is a picture book author, published poetess and a primary school and special education teacher. Her favourite place is at the beach, soaking up the sunshine and being surrounded by ocean water. She loves reading, but wishes she had more time to read the endless mountains of books piling up! For inspiration to write, Linda draws upon the love of life's beautiful and varied experiences involving her family and friends. She also loves writing fiction and writing about social and mental heath issues. She lives on Sydney's Northern Beaches with her husband, two sons and a dog named Cookie.

Instagram: @lindalokheeauthor
Website: www.lindalokhee.com

Valerie

Valerie is a lover of words, expression and unity. She lives in Ireland with her loving husband and son. She is one half of @poetspotlight who curated and edited this book.

You can find more from this poet at @beingyoubeingtrue on Instagram.

Sky Rose

Sky Rose is a mother, poet, author, youtuber, creatrix and entrepreneur. She lives in the UK with her partner and their three children. Her writing is a blend of spirituality, nature, equality and empowerment, with a dash of fantasy and magick. She is also one half of @poetspotlight, who curated and edited this book. You can find more of her writings on Instagram @skyroseheywood

Printed in Great Britain
by Amazon